Maintenance Turns to the Computer

Maintenance Turns to the Computer

by James K. Hildebrand

CAHNERS BOOKS, Division of Cahners Publishing Company, Inc.
89 Franklin Street, Boston, Massachusetts   02110

International Standard Book Number: 0–8436–0808–0
Library of Congress Catalog Card Number: 75–109095

Printed in the United States of America.
The Maple Press Company, York, Pennsylvania, U.S.A.

Contents

Introduction

Maintenance is big business. An estimated 25 billion dollars is spent annually to keep our industrial and service facilities operating. The need for sophisticated maintenance management is obvious.

Industry is starting to "round out" the top of the progress curve for scientific production management. But efforts to control maintenance activities have lagged, mainly because maintenance usually has been considered a necessary spender of funds and producer of nothing.

This attitude is changing. Labor costs have risen to a point where maintenance man-hours are meaningful as a major expense. In a reverse sense, maintenance can contribute to the profit picture by more efficiently managing its operation and reducing the "expense" term in the profit equation.

Recent surveys have indicated that, where management control is applied, results are good. Maintenance productivity with no form of control program is about 30%–40%. With the initiation of a basic control system, productivity jumps to 50%–60%; with the introduction of engineered performance standards, possibly to 75%; with work improvement, to 80%; and, with wage incentives, as high as to 90%.

What, then, is the maintenance problem? Why are many maintenance departments operated at such low levels of proficiency?

Many plants have their maintenance costs structured in very broad, general terms. Their managements know how much is spent on maintenance generally, but not specifically where and how it is being spent. While industrial accounting systems are finely geared to pinpoint every phase of "cost to manufacture," "cost of materials," and "cost of selling," "costs to maintain all these facilities and equipment" are usually lumped together in the expense ledger and cause only momentary head shaking at board meetings.

Progressive companies are asking, "Where is this maintenance money being spent?" and, more importantly, "How can this expenditure be reduced?" As a result, systems are being devised to identify cost sources.

Because management at the decision-making level cannot hope to be familiar with every piece of equipment in the organization, systems are being developed to identify the availability and cost characteristics of each piece of equipment. Before an intelligent decision can be made about the degree of maintenance required for any given area or equipment, a maintenance manager must supply current, accurate data, such as hours operated, maintenance costs, and downtime priority.

From these basic requirements have evolved some basic data collecting systems. At inception, most systems involve some sort of work card which combines hours, machines, and materials. This, followed by considerable manual posting, yields some cost data.

However, manual systems are handicapped by slow reaction time, clerical costs, and lack of detail. Because these systems tend to be either too general or too limited in scope, a maintenance manager is continually bothered by detail and worry about pertinent information being overlooked.

Where does this lead? Our requirement is for an all-inclusive, detailed, but highlighted data collection and *presentation* system which will allow the modern maintenance manager to get on top of his facility and stay there; a system that will relieve the burden of detail watching; a system that will allow the manager to be relatively free for constructive and corrective thinking. This managerial utopia can best be approached by an electronic data processing system utilizing computer memory and flexibility.

The development and utilization of such a system is what this book is about (see Figure I-1). It presents a topically arranged series of articles concerned mainly with how to develop and use a data collection and presentation system — not merely general reports on what others have done. Most of the programs and concepts are original with the

Fig. I –1: Information Flow: What This Book Is About*

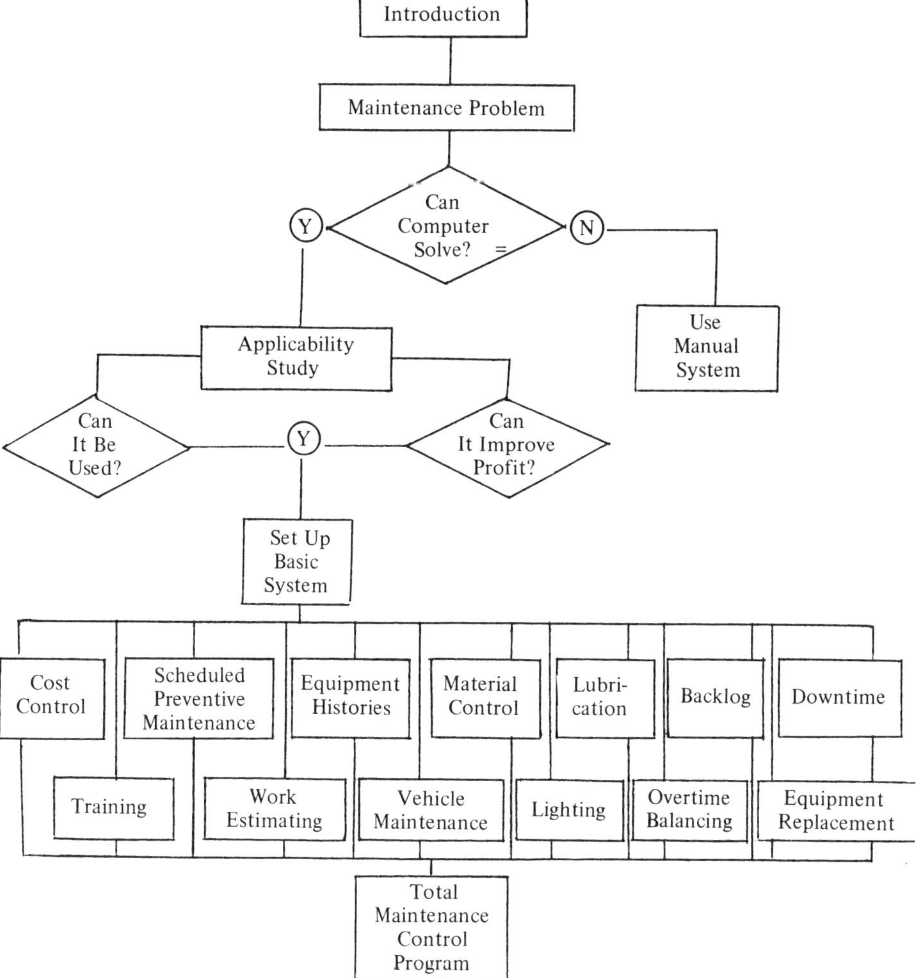

*This type of summation will be used throughout the book. It is the basic system definition method used by systems engineers and programmers.

author and are currently in use in his maintenance department. Actual experience is supplemented with procedures and theories gleaned from extensive research of pertinent trade publications and other source material.

The first section of the book presents a general discussion of the maintenance problem, followed by a thorough study of computer applicability, where computer systems can be used and if we actually need them to improve our profit contribution.

Following this is a series of chapters, each dealing with a separate phase of maintenance management, such as preventive maintenance, scheduling, and lubrication. In each of these chapters both the problem and a procedure which will bring about a solution are discussed. Then, the program will be fitted to the existing EDP (electronic data processing) program. As will be seen, many of these programs are interrelated, having a common base in the basic data input card or work order card.

Included in many chapters are "case studies" dealing with the preceding chapters' topics. These are actual work situations and will greatly assist the reader in envisioning the circumstances to which data processing can be applied. Many of these dramas are drawn from actual experience. They will help the reader to remember the practicality of our subject: Unless the discussion is tied to actual application, it is very possible for the small plant maintenance manager to feel that sophisticated systematization is beyond the scope of his operation.

Nothing can be further from the truth. The procedures described in this book can be applied in the smallest maintenance department. Our application studies dramatize situations all too familiar to any maintenance-oriented reader, allowing him to identify with the problem and to envision the data processing solution in his plant.

This book attempts to counteract the current trend which supports elaborate systems perfectly applicable only in large production facilities. While the procedures herein are equally sophisticated, they are written with the small department in mind. The programs discussed are applicable to any small plant. These programs will, of course, find equal, if not even more spectacular success in the large maintenance department as well.

Maintenance Turns
to the Computer

I. The Maintenance Problem

"How come maintenance didn't take care of that?" How typical a question that is. An age-old verse expands this thought:

> "I'm not allowed to run the train
> Or see how fast 'twill go.
> I ain't allowed to let off steam
> Or make the whistle blow.
> I cannot exercise control
> Or even ring the bell.
> But let the damn thing jump the track
> And see who catches hell."

Herein lies our problem: maintenance prominence. We are coping with a precedent that has long placed maintenance at the bottom of the ladder. Besides being a troublesome expense to the thrift-oriented treasurer, maintenance has been the fall guy for many a production head when things go wrong. Maintenance encounters top management only when there is an immediate, serious problem and the atmosphere borders on frantic; or when some large expenditure is necessary which won't contribute anything real to profit.

Maintenance, therefore, operates in a negative atmosphere. Our greatest achievement is correcting a wrong situation, often not correcting it to the complete satisfaction of everyone involved, and usually working with the feeling that we should have prevented the error in the first place.

This problem of negative work atmosphere has many aspects in addition to the relative position of maintenance management. We must examine the effect on our maintenance man, because he, after all, will play an important part in the ultimate solution, and we must understand his position thoroughly in order to gain his cooperation.

What sort of effect does the negative atmosphere have on our maintenance man? This will vary, of course, with the plant and the man involved, but, generally, he will not be inspired working under the old "Hey, Joe" system of assignment and control. He certainly must wonder about the importance of *his* efforts when he sees his fellow workers in production working under the most modern system of control. Higher wage rates and extra overtime are of prime importance to most men, but these advantages are of a different type and do not affect his day-to-day work.

The point is that this psychological difference will have an adverse effect on our maintenance man, who, by nature of his skills, is often more sensitive than others and, also, takes exceptional pride in his work.

It is, therefore, especially important that we establish a well-organized, tightly controlled operation in which the maintenance man can take part with pride and with a feeling of solidarity with the activities of his supervisors and department.

The other facet of the maintenance problem is the effect of maintenance department status on production workers and supervision. Anyone connected with maintenance knows that a substantial portion of repair problems is due to indifferent operation of the equipment. If maintenance is regarded as the company dumping grounds, production (especially front line) supervision is likely to dump the problem — and the responsibility — back in the lap of maintenance. This problem is expressed often at gatherings of maintenance managers: "If only they'd listened; I told them what was going to happen."

CASE STUDY I: "GENTLEMEN, WE MUST CLOSE THE DOORS."

C. M. Foundry was having profit difficulties, as have many small foundries in recent years. Total production was off, but fixed costs remained the same, and so the company was operating at a loss. The sales potential was there, but poor customer service and broken delivery promises had chased away some good customers.

As the company continued to lose money, the absentee owners brought in a cost control expert to attempt to solve the problem. This man, quite obviously, knew little of production requirements. His method of operation was to attack General and Administrative (G & A). One of the first to go was the plant maintenance engineer. "We just can't afford a plant engineer" was the reasoning.

Now this plant engineer had been fighting a losing battle up to this time because expenditures for equipment maintenance and updating had not been made. As profits started to shrink, this was the first cost area to be reduced.

This reduction started the vicious cycle. As less money was spent on maintenance materials and as the department functioned without professional leadership, the plant's equipment ran steadily downhill. As equipment downtime increased, productive capacity was further lessened. With continually reduced ability to produce sales dollars, about the only maintenance material the plant purchased was baling wire.

Tom, the Maintenance Foreman, was on the carpet continually for downtime problems. His requests for repair expenditures were shrugged off. "There just wasn't enough money." The old millwright could see what was happening, but he was at a loss as to how to present the whole picture to a financially oriented management.

One day, the inevitable meeting took place. The general manager held a plant-wide meeting and announced: "Gentlemen, we must close the doors." A group of senior employees had seen this coming; using funds accumulated when the company was profitable, they arranged to pick up the pieces out of bankruptcy court and to put the company back together. Leaning heavily on sales potential, capital improvement funds were borrowed and much of the run-down equipment was rebuilt or replaced.

Needless to say, a firm, on-going maintenance program was one of the first orders of business. With reliable equipment to sustain production, the company, after a time, began to prosper.

The object lesson of this case study is the critical importance of production equipment maintenance, particularly in an operation like a foundry, where there are relatively few pieces of capital equipment. Without the flexibility of an assembly plant with rows of presses, maintenance priority is very heavy in those few vital pieces.

Fig. 1-1: Information Flow: The Maintenance Problem

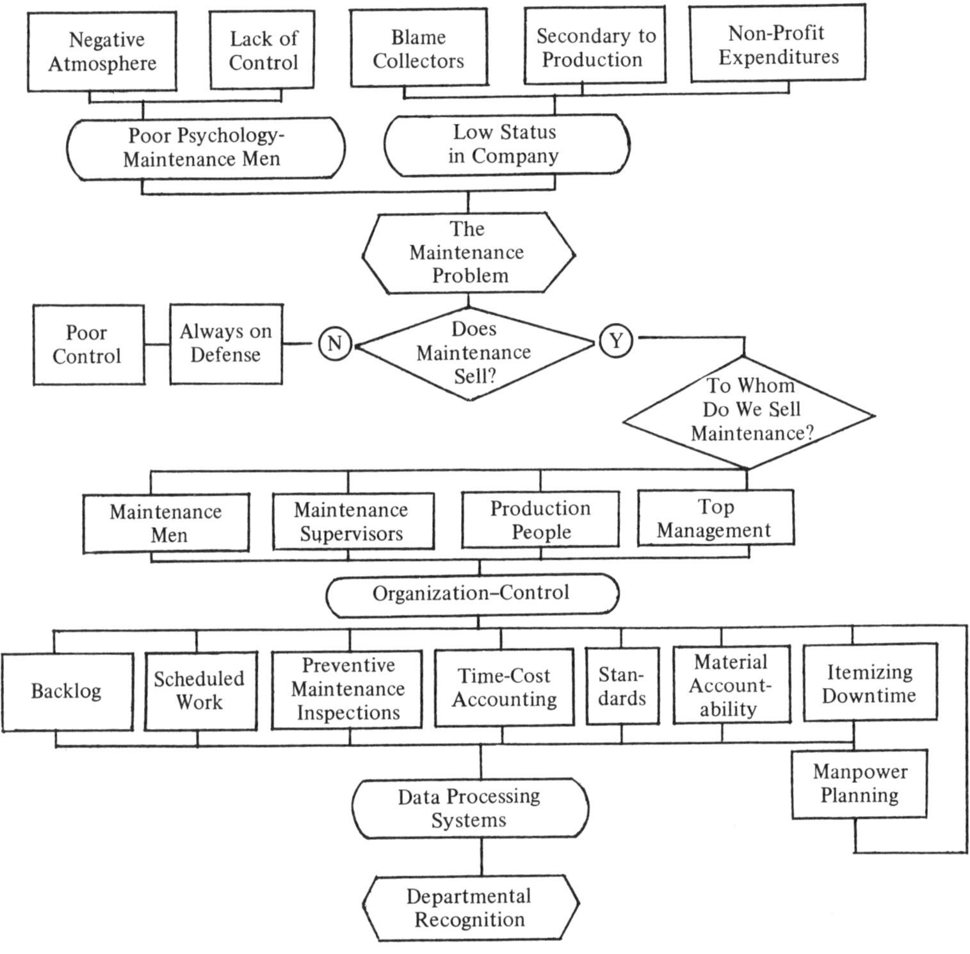

The Need to Sell Maintenance Control

Now that we have better defined the maintenance problem, let us delve into the internal workings of our department and see just why our product — maintenance — doesn't sell as we would like it to.

Lack of control is certainly a factor. We are moved to action by outside causes more often than is necessary. As a result, it is difficult for maintenance management to really get "on top" of the job. Let's look a little closer at each of these "product defects."

Lack of control, in most cases, really means lack of planning. We rely too much on our ability and the ability of our men to notice jobs that need to be done. We are not in a position to exhibit control when we are asked, "When is the last time you checked that machine, and what did you find?" and our answer is, "Well, let me try to remember"; or, if, in a repeat breakdown, we want to know who was on the job the first time and our foreman's reply is, "Well, now, I think it was . . ." While these ludicrous examples are not entirely typical, they are examples of weaknesses which are present to some extent in most of our departments.

A problem-oriented maintenance department whose men and supervisors come to work wondering, "What on earth will go wrong today?" is very much like a battle troop dug into a defensive position wondering what the enemy will throw at them next. Such a department, where the problems determine the course of action, never seem to get caught up in their work but, rather, just shift position to cover the next breakdown. The answer, again, lies in a systematized approach to the job.

Let's shift our attention from personnel organization to the monetary aspect of our business. While efficient use of personnel is an economic function, we are also concerned with the dollars spent on materials. Most companies have (or certainly should have) some means of knowing how much money is spent on maintenance. And many companies have systems which tell how much money is spent on individual pieces of equipment. But, how many companies have a method to determine how much *should* have been spent and where *too much* is being spent?

How to Sell Maintenance Control

Having defined the problem and examined how it affects our operation, let's look at what is needed to rehabilitate maintenance and so make it saleable to our own men, to production people, and to top management.

The maintenance man will work harder in a better organized, systematized department. The organization program will include more scheduled work, preventive maintenance inspections, specific accounting of the maintenance man's time, standards toward which to work, and material accountability. The maintenance man can assume rightful pride in his work and the equipment when the production foreman tells the production man to: "Shut down your machine; maintenance is here for a scheduled check." This places him in an offensive position regarding equipment failure rather than having to defensively sit back and wait for trouble. This man will know his efforts are closely scrutinized when he is called in and told that "records show" that he has been consistently over or under the standards; or, that his particular area of work has shown a 32% decrease in downtime and 15% decrease in materials during the past year. His feeling of achievement will be enhanced when he can walk into the maintenance office, pull an equipment record to review a problem area and see the machine's history, which he has helped to record.

The production man will sit up and take notice when he sees his machine lubricated and inspected at regular intervals; he will become aware of downtime when the review board finds him negligent in "that carriage gear failure the other night." The production foreman will better appreciate the maintenance department when he sees the maintenance man hustle in to his department to get the job done within standards, instead of talking to the operator on #57 as he previously had done. The foreman will notice, too, that maintenance replaced that leaky coolant hose on #144 that his men had been after him to report — must have been on that preventive maintenance check last night. And, how about Franz finding that sheared key so fast yesterday? — said it happened the same way two years ago this June.

Top management — who must, of course, be sold on the program initially — will be delighted to see the graphic and tabular results of the maintenance operation. Much of their reluctance to give sufficient attention to maintenance in the past was due to lack of understanding. Presenting the historical facts of our system, including itemized costs, downtime, manpower utilization, and backlog, will make top management much more cognizant of maintenance as an operating department rather than as just an expensive place to call when a light burns out.

Top management will notice, too, a large decrease in the frequency of production heads screaming for the scalps of maintenance because of unexpected downtime. With the systematized approach to maintenance, top management learn they are dealing with a professional manager, one to whom they had better listen the next time equipment replacement is discussed.

CASE STUDY II: "LET MAINTENANCE DO IT; THEY HAVE PLENTY OF TIME."

Jack Warden, as maintenance manager in a large stamping and assembly plant, was faced with a considerable increase in maintenance labor costs and no improvement in an already high downtime figure. Jack had worked hard to develop a well-skilled and in-plant-experienced work force. Most of them were on area assignments, responsible to that area's production foreman. The central shop repaired components and supplied back-up assistance where needed.

Other than a well-disciplined lubrication plan, maintenance was carried out almost entirely on a breakdown basis. Some past attempts at a planned schedule of maintenance work had bogged down, principally because it was operated through the production foremen. These people, obviously, were reluctant to shut down equipment for "needless" maintenance. The total number of maintenance men required was justified in everyone's mind because of the very frequent breakdowns and the manpower "insurance" necessary to cover simultaneous malfunctions.

The plant operated on two shifts, with some departments on three. Saturday was a full maintenance day and was used principally for going back and doing completely what was done part way during the week to keep equipment running.

A work sampling of maintenance personnel revealed a 35% productivity. The prime offenders were "awaiting assignment" or had "personal" delays. In his subjective summation, the industrial engineer responsible for the study described a work force without purpose or direction.

This was all Jack the maintenance manager needed to finally crack the production foreman's hold on maintenance activities and to develop a good preventive maintenance program. He compiled a report, with the following proposals as keys to his recommendation:

1. Combine several maintenance areas with maintenance foreman assigned;
2. Develop preventive maintenance checklists and schedules; and
3. Secure full cooperation from production in scheduling equipment downtime for preventive maintenance.

The above steps will accomplish:

a. decreased downtime after preventive maintenance has time for full effect;
b. relieve production foremen of direct maintenance supervision;
c. make better use of maintenance men's time; and,
d. as breakdowns come under control, possibly reduce maintenance force, depending on manpower required to operate preventive maintenance program.

Plant management finally realized this was probably the only way to maintain reliably operational equipment and lent the new program full support. Results, of course, did not come right away, nor without considerable difficulty, but the program did satisfy the original goals.

The greatest value of the new program, not totally unexpected, was a far better working maintenance crew. Good mechanics and electricians became good productive workers. They now had a stake in the operation because it was their equipment to inspect and keep operative. Posting of departmental downtime created competition within the department. An *esprit de corps* was generated which had not been possible under partial production supervision. The men were able to get on top of their jobs instead of always being behind with breakdowns.

A work sampling taken a year later showed an actual work percentage of 65% — almost double the previous study. The subjective comment this time described a "controlled and purposeful" working group.

In this age of high labor cost, it is much to management's advantage to secure the highest productivity from its "fixed" indirect costs. The psychological advantage of purposeful work controls designed to encourage individual contribution cannot be overestimated in achieving this productivity goal.

The Obvious Solution

We know the problem, its effects, and, now, the results of its solution. What is the means by which we can gain the solution?

First, let's talk about our solution — the systematized approach. What is it, really? It is a concept, an outlook, a thought process that should be considered for every type of problem. Specifically, it is the application of a system, or set procedure, to every type of repetitive situation. It is a means of control which the maintenance man and maintenance supervisor can use to insure complete maintenance coverage of plant and equipment.

There are two main phases of the systematized approach: scheduling and information. Scheduling is the input to the system; information, the output, or results. The many categories of these two main phases will be discussed in detail in later chapters. They include scheduling of work, preventive maintenance, lubrication, cost data, standards, and backlog, among others.

It is obvious by now that there must be some force, external to the maintenance department, which collects, organizes, and disseminates maintenance data and information. This external factor is, of course, an electronic data processing system (EDP).

In the following chapters, we will explain several maintenance systems and their affiliations with EDP and the computer. Once the computer enters the picture, it opens up other system possibilities not possible before. And, in developing systems and programs, we find our thinking guided by how the computer can assist and be utilized.

II. Where Is the Computer Applicable?

As a maintenance department matures and becomes more sophisticated, it will make more and more use of "that machine." This chapter mentions, generally, the many programs that can be assisted by EDP. But we must begin with an analysis of the need and economic justification for computer use. The specific advantages of EDP and a plan for the small firm that cannot justify buying its own EDP equipment are also given.

What Problem Are We Attempting to Solve?

The very first step in considering any systematized program, computerized or not, is to clearly define the problem or objectives. Once having defined the problem, we work back: first to the basic requirement, naming the information necessary to solve the problem; then to finding the sources of that information; then extracting the information from the sources; and, finally, collecting and disseminating the data. Figure 2-1 charts this thinking process with a basic example dealing with cost control. While this method provides only a very general solution to the problem, it does show how the initial problem definition leads to the steps contributing to its solution.

Do We Really Need the Services of a Computer?

While a simple "yes" or "no" will answer this question, the reasoning that leads to the answer can be complex and, often, not specific as to the economics involved. Robert Cash writes:

Fig. 2-1: Defining the Problem

1. What is the problem?	1. Secure better knowledge of maintenance costs.
2. What information is needed?	2. Labor costs, material costs, administrative costs.
3. What are the sources of this information?	3. The maintenance man, stockroom disbursing, accounting department.

4. How do we extract this information?
  a. Labor costs.
	4. From:
	  a. Maintenance man fills out card showing time spent and on which piece of equipment or service.

b. Material costs.	b. Record of new items purchased and expensed against equipment; also, a card filled out for items taken from stockroom not previously expensed.
c. Administrative costs. 5. Collect and disseminate the data.	c. Salary records. 5. A tabulating function is needed to organize the input labor and material usage cards and to publish them in reports designed to isolate various areas of cost responsibility.

The costs of equipment, programming, system analysis, and daily operations must be weighed against the ability to make decisions from the read-out obtained. In short, can all costs be offset by decisions that are only or primarily possible through the reports obtained? If you are already getting enough data to make the same decisions as quickly as necessary, then you really do not need the computer. Recognition of this point can save the company and organization many dollars and headaches in the long run.

We should compare the costs of providing a determined level of input data accuracy with the accuracy requirements for the output data. That is, the time consumed by the mechanic, the clerk, or the supervisor who supplies data or fills out reporting forms (cards) and the time required to monitor these data should be related to how much accuracy you need to be able to make sound judgments about the activity being measured.[1]

Mr. Cash's point about whether the value of computer data will be an improvement over existing control measures is the true measure of the need for a computer. Justification on the basis of the elimination of

1. Robert G. Cash, "Computerized Control of Maintenance," *Techniques of Plant Engineering and Maintenance,* Volume XVI (New York: Clapp and Poliak, Inc., 1965), p. 21.

a clerk is not adequate. (In most cases, anyway, a maintenance clerk is necessary for work order processing, phone service, and a multitude of filing duties.)

Justification for computer use, if it must be in economic terms, begins with a positive need for the increased control measures and records afforded by the system. Once this need is shown, calculating the number of additional clerks required to provide the same information manually yields a more concrete justification.

Of even greater impact, though less definite than administrative savings, are some estimated savings in incidents revealed by the proposed system. Examples of these are recognition of a repeat write-up causing considerable downtime, or, a wrong part revealed by high replacement incidence on a material report.

The Computer Can't Do It All.

In further appraising the merits of a computer, we must be entirely cognizant of the fact that the computer is limited to producing evidence of a bad situation. It can't initiate the action required to correct the situation.

The facts and figures generated as the end result of use of the system do not in themselves control. They are merely starting points for management action. It is possible to have numerous schedules, management reports, charts, graphs, but unless management action is taken to solve the problems indicated in these data collection devices, business will continue as usual and be uncontrolled except for routine management action required by day to day circumstances. Forms, documents, reports, and records are merely the framework upon which a series of facts are built. The control of the maintenance department comes from intelligent analysis and management action taken after considering these facts.

There is some element of control in nearly every action that management performs but scientific control involves three steps: planning, performing the plan, and management action and reaction. Successful maintenance management control requires use of reports as 'score cards' and vigorous follow-up action to counteract any delaying operations in the maintenance department.[2]

2. Bernard T. Lewis, *Controlling Maintenance Costs* (Bureau of Business Practices, Waterford, Connecticut, 1964), p. 111.

CASE STUDY III: "TOO MANY REPORTS."

Tomlin Industries was a sophisticated group of industrial holdings supplying support equipment to the general aerospace industry. It was well equipped and well staffed in data processing and systems. This department turned out a myriad of production and financial reports to corporate and divisional operating heads.

Since all efforts were aimed at growth expansion, little emphasis was placed on profit development. The percent of earnings was not keeping up with the tremendous increase in revenues. When certain anti-trust proceedings showed acquisition plans, management returned its direction to operations and construction of a stronger profit and cash base.

Understandably, over the past few years, monies had been diverted from equipment renovation and used for acquisition. The resulting condition of physical assets and the reflection on profits are obvious.

The corporation brought in Bob Rasset to head up a new staff function: facilities management. His first task was to establish control procedures and cost collection data. With corporate interest shifted to maintenance problems, Bob's work became a crash project.

In a few months' time, EDP systems were established for labor and material cost segregation, downtime, preventive maintenance, lubrication, and backlog. In fact, the initial, unrefined reports were rolling out of the EDP section and stacking up on the desks of several supervisors. Bob became concerned with productivity of the maintenance force and started immediately on a basic standards program.

Eight months passed after the new reports were generated; a very patient management noted no improvement in downtime or material costs and a slight increase in labor costs. Bob was called on the carpet, and, while he was complimented on the splendid control system he had established, he was given to the end of his first year to show some improvement in labor costs and downtime.

Bob was quite angry with himself for allowing this sort of ultimatum to have been issued. Pretty obviously, he had become too involved in procedures and not enough with results. By neglecting to realize that reports alone do not provide improvement, he had placed a very good control system in jeopardy. His meetings with his supervisors were, of course, concerned with the reports and their unsatisfactory contents. Results were distributed, with some general word about improvement. He recalled having been somewhat annoyed at the indifference and impatience displayed by some of his foremen.

Rasset figured that the preventive maintenance and lubrication programs, which had only been in operation for a few months, would start to show a return soon *if* they were operating properly. The people problem was quite another matter, and Bob initiated a series of individual meetings with his superintendent and foremen.

Almost immediately, the answer became clear. The only attention the supervisors gave the reports was to carry them from Bob's office to a desk drawer. The maintenance men, who, typically, believe a pencil has no place in a tool box, were rebelling against the additional "paperwork" required by the labor reporting card. Bob had defined the problems very carefully, but had been totally unsuccessful in solving them. The reason was twofold: One was the old management nemesis in a typical "trouble by absence" role — communication; the other was lack of follow-up. He now faced a really tough job of correcting these deficiencies — a job which would have been much easier at the outset of his program.

Concentrating on his superintendent, Bob went back to the beginning and showed the advantages of each report. This time, though, he concentrated on soliciting the supervisors' inquiries with, "Now, that you've had a chance to see the system, what can we do to improve it and sell it to the men?"

He had some simple transparencies assembled, showing the final reports of costs, downtime, and backlog. Meetings of the maintenance work force were scheduled, and three of the foremen presented the explanation. Bob merely added a few comments at these sessions and was pleased with the reaction of the men to the foremen's involvement with the new program.

In these sessions, a tradesman was asked to come up and initiate a labor reporting card. Through a block diagram presentation (such as those seen throughout this book), the progress of the card was traced to its contribution to each applicable report. Then, the reports themselves were displayed. At each step, a reference was made to the implication for the individual maintenance man. Examples were:

— downtime report, showing up repeated nuisance jobs requiring engineering modifications;
— cost report, describing cost of machine the maintenance men said should be replaced two years ago;
— backlog report, assisting scheduling in the allotment of overtime; and
— mention of yet-to-come training and overtime equalization reports.

With the basic communication established as it should have been initially, Bob went to work on following up and actually using the reports. The first step was to shelve a few of the later, more detailed reports and to concentrate on the basic ones. Combining a sporting approach with a dead serious one, he erected a departmental scorecard in the central maintenance shop. Each craft section was listed by standing according to percent improvement in the areas of labor cost and backlog. An overall departmental downtime figure was displayed; a half day off with pay was awarded to the section with the most improvement each quarter. A company contribution in the name of the maintenance department was to be made at each year's end to the local children's home for each month's reduction in downtime.

To put more teeth in the program, a stand-up briefing was scheduled each month; each foreman showing negative progress in any reporting area was required to explain in depth the circumstances resulting in his poor showing. This, alone, brought the reports out of the desk drawers and home at night for further review and understanding. To prod the non-sporting members of the maintenance force, the old repeat-write-up form was dug out and brought into perspective, with space for downtime hours lost and maintenance labor cost added to the slip that was placed in the man's personnel jacket for a year's time.

The effect of these simple "people" programs was overwhelming. Bob Rasset now had a results-oriented maintenance team, with the reports properly placed in a secondary position — merely reporting the efforts of the department. Additional reports brought back into action were absorbed without difficulty.

The twofold lesson here is:

1. Sell the program to the operating people.
2. Initiate solid follow-up procedures in order to make use of control reports generated by the EDP system.

Any good systems man can develop EDP controls and procedures, but it takes a real manager to make them work!

What Are the Advantages of EDP?

Now that we have looked at specific problem definitions leading to a computer system, decided whether or not we really should consider a system, and are prepared to make use of the results if we do install a system, we are better able to evaluate the advantages of EDP. We will weigh these advantages by comparing them to some manual system.

We assume that the systematized approach is already accepted and we are searching for the best method of implementation.

Low Cost: We will eliminate some clerical cost by using the punched card and electronic data processing system to provide the same information now recorded manually. To provide manually the amount of control data possible with EDP would require even more clerical cost.

Accuracy: The human error element is reduced with EDP. It virtually eliminates any error in process (key punch error is very slight) and allows us to concentrate all efforts on insuring the accuracy of the input data. Most of this kind of error has been eliminated through scientifically designed input cards and simple-to-follow coding systems.

Completeness: EDP not only provides the digestion and logical presentation of great volumes of data in a particular area of control, it stores the critical data (within the reasonable limits of storage capacity) and can use it in a completely different presentation at a later time. This capability is inconceivable in manual record keeping. This advantage is analogous to the well-known ability of the computer to solve in seconds mathematical problems that could take weeks of manual calculations. With the computer, we will be able to know much more about our plant and equipment than we possibly could by any other means.

Speed: A vast amount of information is available to us in many forms, very quickly.

Versatility: This is a corollary to completeness. The fact that this wealth of information can be stored electronically and brought out for use in other forms to solve related problems is a key feature of EDP.

Automatic Schedule Control: The ability of this system to receive a program of scheduled work, preventive inspections, routine adjustments, etc., and to balance this workload and publish periodic schedules is a very important asset — one which relieves maintenance management of great concern over whether everything is getting done. (Specifics of schedule control are covered in later chapters.)

Routine Cost Identification: Another corollary to completeness is the ability of our EDP system to identify costs — some of them considerable — of routine repetitive tasks which might otherwise be taken for granted and not considered for cost reduction.

What Types of Maintenance Jobs Can Be Handled by the Computer?

Up to now, we have talked much in generalities about systems and computers. Before we cover the basic system to be used, we should make brief mention of those problem areas in which we can gain assistance from the computer.

1. *Cost Control:* This includes complete labor and material costs allocated by machine, area, account, or whatever classification is desired. We can read periodic and accumulative costs and monthly departmental trends.
2. *Scheduling and Preventive Maintenance:* These tasks are easily assigned to the computer and it will accomplish a better job of workload balancing than can be done manually. In addition to planning preventive maintenance, the computer is adept at scheduling repetitive block projects utilizing pre-printed work cards.
3. *System Histories:* Historical records are of paramount importance in the operation of a maintenance department. The computer can provide a printed history for each piece of equipment, showing repair incidence, failure type, parts replaced, whether repair was scheduled, or breakdown.
4. *Work Standards:* These can be used for performance checks, planning, and scheduling. We can generate computer reports which show standard versus actual times by individual, by craft, or by project. The computer is valuable in compiling and updating the standards.
5. *Materials Control:* Inventory control, including re-order points, levels, and economic order quantities, is one of the original commercial uses of computers. Standard cost computation and periodically printed stock lists and catalogs make the computer invaluable in this area.
6. *Lubrication:* "The operation on which the plant runs" is particularly adaptable to EDP due to the tremendous volume of items to be scheduled. Weekly schedules or individual operation cards can be used and either system can be scheduled in such a way as to assure complete lubrication coverage.
7. *Downtime:* Monthly reports showing total downtime by machine and cumulative reports showing any machine's downtime history are easily available under the computer system.
8. *Training Control:* A much needed plan to control and account for training efforts is available. Reports will show training time spent

and what is still to be accomplished by which man and in which area of training.

9. *Vehicle Costs:* This area is easily adaptable to machine control and we can determine fuel and repair costs by vehicle and by hours used. We can establish programs to predict component replacement and even vehicle replacement.

10. *Lighting:* A taken-for-granted expense is minimized by special programs which tell us about service costs and re-lamping — if, and how often.

11. *Backlog:* This presentation shows in which craft areas the biggest backlogs are. It can also provide priority and date-sorted listings of all backlog work.

12. *Overtime Balancing:* All preferential treatment charges can be thwarted with this report which lists each man and his accumulated overtime by craft group. It can also differentiate between Sunday and doubletime work.

Maintenance Can Only Contribute to Computer Justification

It is apparent, from the maintenance areas listed above, that, while the computer would be of immeasurable assistance in managing a maintenance department, its needs would not, in themselves, create enough time demand to justify the computer. It is also apparent that any company that is progressive enough to consider a computer for maintenance work will probably already have a machine or will be considering using it for other accounting and production functions.

The point is that any maintenance manager in a company without a computer should organize his selling approach to top management in conjunction with other using departments. It is entirely possible that the company has already considered a computer, primarily for accounting and production, and this additional benefit in maintenance may be enough to force a positive decision.

It is obvious that the very near future will bring some sort of computer facility to all but the smallest manufacturing and service firms.

This situation is analogous to today's almost universal use of some form of electronic data processing equipment for accounting and payroll procedures.

For the company that is just too small to purchase its own computer or one that would like to sample computer results, there are an increasing number of computer centers where computer time can be leased. These centers, located in all large cities and in many small ones, have trained personnel to assist in setting up programs. These programs can be organized to run a few hours per month at a relatively nominal charge. Billing is usually monthly, on an hourly rate basis.

Leasing computer time would normally restrict the company to monthly or weekly runs of a definite program, such as preventive maintenance schedules and cost sheets. The leasing method handicaps the company in the type of runs required on a daily basis and special reports needed on short notice.

III. Installing
the Basic System

The starting point of our data processing system is the data input mechanism. This chapter describes the mechanism and shows how to begin implementation.

The labor reporting card, or work order card, is the most important single item in the program. It is from this card that we gather the labor hours spent in the many activities we will attempt to control. There are two different types of cards in general use: a card used just to record time spent and used in conjunction with a separate work order card; and a single card, combining the scheduling and hours reporting function. Both accomplish basically the same result. We will discuss each in some detail later.

What is the card actually for? On it are recorded the man-hours spent by an individual on a specific job or in a specific activity. These man-hours are then combined by the EDP equipment to produce the many reports necessary for control. The hours are recorded on the card by the maintenance man, either by hand or by time clock.

Certain data fields are common to any labor reporting card and these are listed and described below.

1. *Activity Identification:* This item describes the activity involved and varies from plant to plant, depending on individual accounting systems. This field includes such titles as account number, shop order number, shop repair account number, and control number.
2. *Machine Number:* This is often the same as the activity number

but, in any event, it is the specific identification code used for a piece of equipment.

3. *Work Order Number:* Identifies that particular job assignment (pre-printed in most cases).

4. *Location:* This is an area or building designation and is necessary only in a large plant.

5. *Description:* This verbal identification of the equipment is indeed optional. In most plants, the machine number suffices, the numbers themselves being coded at least by plant area or type of manufacturing activity.

6. *Employee Name:* There is one card per employee per job.

7. *Employee Clock Number:* Self-explanatory.

8. *Craft Designation:* This is used primarily to facilitate backlog reports by craft area, but it also allows cost reports by craft area.

9. *Description of Work Required:* This information is pre-printed in the case of preventive maintenance and scheduled work; it is written in for emergency and breakdown jobs.

10. *Trouble Code:* This code is used to describe the problem; it abbreviates the bulky narrative which would otherwise be required in the machine run-outs of the history of a piece of equipment over a long period of time.

11. *Action Code:* This describes the action taken. Examples would be: tightened, inspected, welded, replaced, etc.

12. *Item Code:* This most nearly describes the part or assembly, such as coolant pump, spindle motor, trolley controller, etc., to which the action applies.

13. *Time Spent:* This is entered in one of two ways. The first uses an "on" and an "off" block, where a man writes or clock-punches his time on and off a job; a timekeeper then computes this time and enters it on the card. The second way has just an "hours" block; the maintenance man must keep track of the time spent on the job and enter this time in the block.

14. *Standard Time:* This is a time span which has been established as standard for a given job or, if it is a one-time or infrequent job, the block is filled with an estimated time. A standard time is suf-

fixed by –S. This allows computer differentiation of standard and estimated times and subsequent individual analysis of each. If more than one man is required, the number is shown as a prefix.

15. *Dates:* Received: when the work order was initiated; scheduled: date when work was scheduled; and completed: date when job was completed.

16. *Requested by:* This identifies the initiator of the work request, which is helpful to the foreman or scheduler in resolving questions about it.

Which is the ideal card layout? Figure 3-1 shows examples of various cards, all different and all serving their particular use well. It is difficult, therefore, to define any one combination of data fields as the optimum data card.

While we have just supported the notion that an input card must be tailored to the system which it serves, the importance of this card cannot be overstressed. It is very likely that the card will undergo several design changes due to different data requirements imposed by additional aspects of each operation as the entire computer control system is developed.

Two Different Input Systems:
Separate versus Combined Cards

We will now discuss the basic differences in input systems mentioned previously. One approach has a card used primarily as a labor hours reporting device. This card identifies the maintenance man, equipment or service account, and refers to a separate work order by number. Hours are normally logged by punching on and off the job with a time clock, or by writing in on and off times, or just the total elapsed time. The total time, if on and off punches are used, is calculated by the foreman or a timekeeper. The advantage of this system is that there is more room on a *separate* work order for writing the work, corrective action, and material required.

There is an additional advantage in a *separate* work order that is worked on at several different times. The work order card can remain

Fig. 3-1: Examples of Input Cards

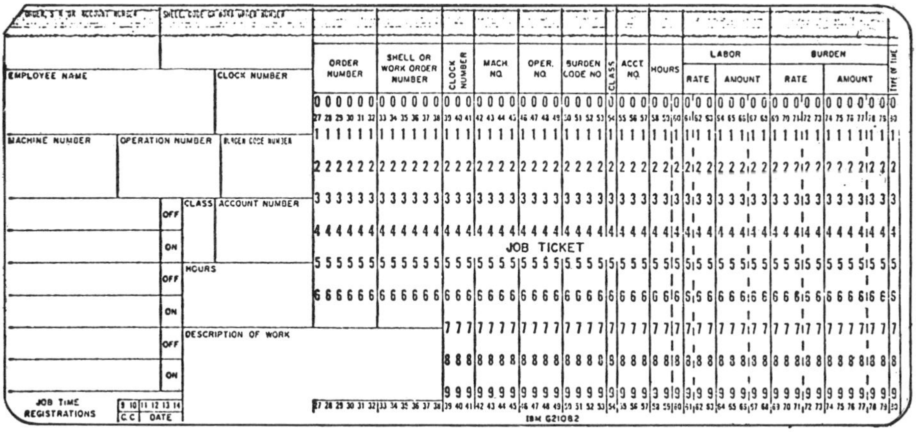

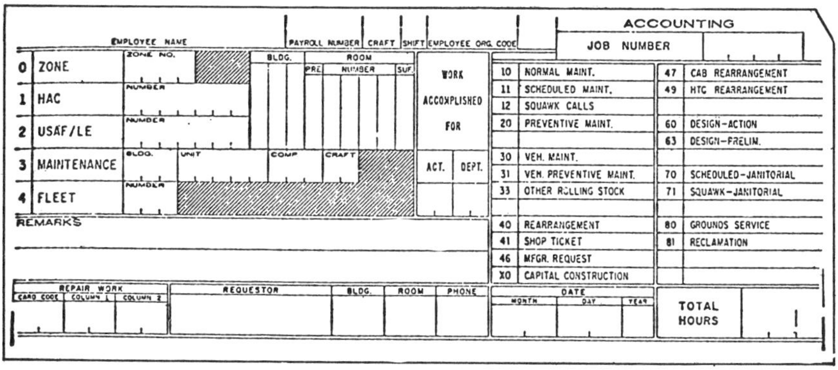

JOB TICKET

	ORDER NUMBER	SHELL OR WORK ORDER NUMBER	CLOCK NUMBER	MACH. NO.	OPER. NO.	BURDEN CODE NO.	CLASS	ACCT. NO.	HOURS	LABOR		BURDEN	
										RATE	AMOUNT	RATE	AMOUNT

EMPLOYEE NAME   CLOCK NUMBER

MACHINE NUMBER   OPERATION NUMBER   BURDEN CODE NUMBER

CLASS   ACCOUNT NUMBER   OFF   ON

HOURS   OFF   ON

DESCRIPTION OF WORK   OFF   ON

JOB TIME REGISTRATIONS   CC   DATE

IBM G21082

ACCOUNTING

EMPLOYEE NAME   PAYROLL NUMBER   CRAFT   SHIFT   EMPLOYEE ORG. CODE

JOB NUMBER

0	ZONE	ZONE NO.	
1	HAC	NUMBER	
2	USAF/LE	NUMBER	
3	MAINTENANCE	BLDG. UNIT COMP CRAFT	
4	FLEET	NUMBER	

BLDG.   ROOM   PRE   NUMBER   SUF.

WORK ACCOMPLISHED FOR   ACT.   DEPT.

Code	Description	Code	Description
10	NORMAL MAINT.	47	CAB REARRANGEMENT
11	SCHEDULED MAINT.	49	HTG. REARRANGEMENT
12	SQUAWK CALLS		
20	PREVENTIVE MAINT.	60	DESIGN-ACTION
		63	DESIGN-PRELIM.
30	VEH. MAINT.		
31	VEH. PREVENTIVE MAINT.	70	SCHEDULED-JANITORIAL
33	OTHER ROLLING STOCK	71	SQUAWK-JANITORIAL
40	REARRANGEMENT	80	GROUNDS SERVICE
41	SHOP TICKET	81	RECLAMATION
46	MFGR. REQUEST		
XO	CAPITAL CONSTRUCTION		

REMARKS

REPAIR WORK   CARD CODE   COLUMN 1   COLUMN 2   REQUESTOR   BLDG.   ROOM   PHONE

DATE   MONTH   DAY   YEAR   TOTAL HOURS

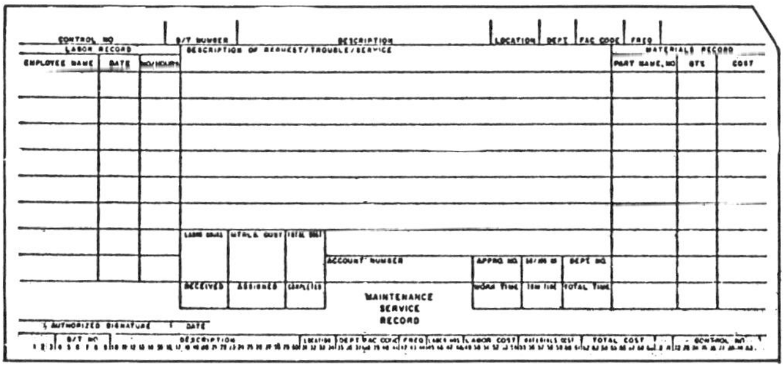

MAINTENANCE SERVICE RECORD

CONTROL NO.   D/T NUMBER   DESCRIPTION   LOCATION   DEPT   FAC CODE   FREQ

LABOR RECORD   DESCRIPTION OF REQUEST/TROUBLE/SERVICE   MATERIAL RECORD

EMPLOYEE NAME   DATE   NO/HOURS   PART NAME, NO.   QTY.   COST

ACCOUNT NUMBER   APPRO NO.   WORK NO.   DEPT NO.

RECEIVED   ASSIGNED   COMPLETED

WORK TIME   TRAVEL TIME   TOTAL TIME

AUTHORIZED SIGNATURE   DATE

Fig. 3–1: Examples of Input Cards (continued)

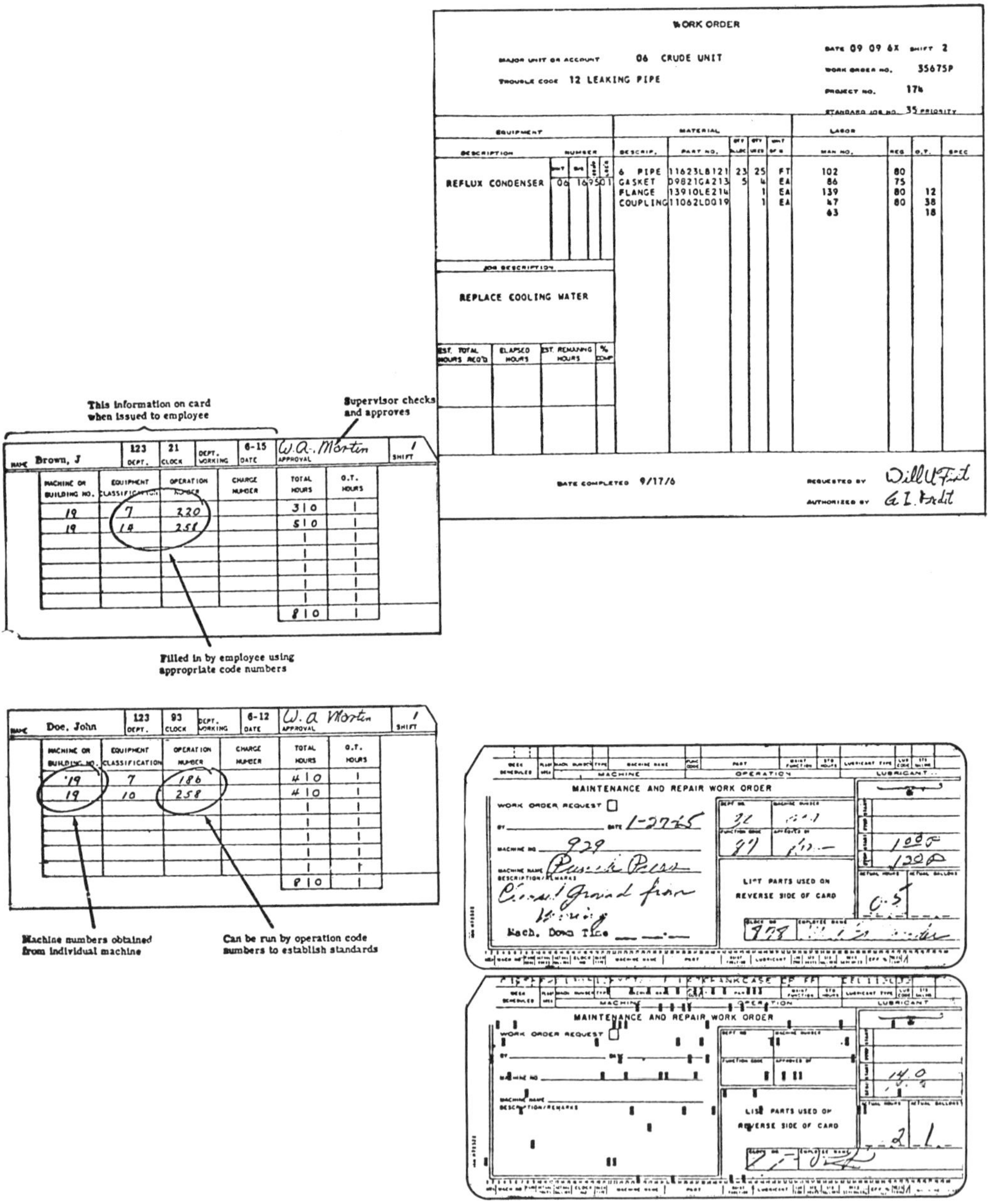

This information on card when issued to employee

Supervisor checks and approves

Filled in by employee using appropriate code numbers

Machine numbers obtained from individual machine

Can be run by operation code numbers to establish standards

Fig. 3–1: Examples of Input Cards (continued)

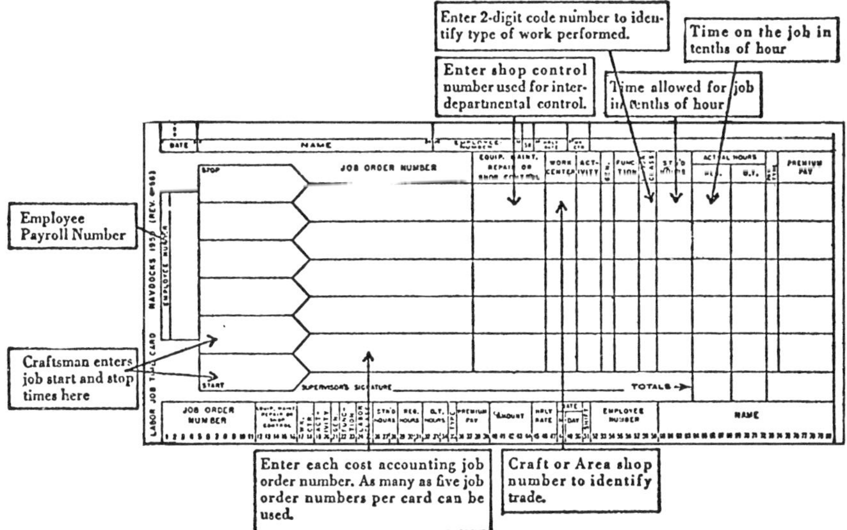

<table>
<tr><td>FORM S-221</td><td colspan="4">PREVENTIVE MAINTENANCE WORK ORDER</td><td>ACCOUNT No ________</td></tr>
</table>

WEEK	JAN.	FEB	MARCH	APRIL	MAY	JUNE	JULY	AUG	SEPT.	OCT.	NOV.	DEC.
	1											

UNIT NAME	DEPT.	CRAFT	UNIT NO.
DRAW FURNACE	SPRING	LUBE	2-5163

— I N S T R U C T I O N S —

BLOWER BEARINGS 2

MOBILUX NO 2 GREASE ZERKS

REEVES DRIVE MOBILUX NO 2 GREASE ZERKS

ASSIGNED TO ________

DATE ________

TIME STOP ________

TIME START ________

TIME ELAPSED ________

WORK ORDER NO.

in the scheduling system while labor reporting cards are generated separately each time work is done. The *combined* work order-labor card, even with several places for job times, is filled sooner and another must be generated. It also presents a problem of accounting for an individual's total daily work hours, if part of his time is logged on an incomplete work order. In a highly EDP-oriented system, however, the card (or a duplicate) can be processed and sent back to the foreman before the start of the next day's work.

The *combined* card has the advantage of reducing paperwork bulk and handling. Every bit of information affiliated with the job is included on one card. This single card eliminates a problem in many shops of incomplete work orders for finished jobs.

This brings us to a perhaps psychological advantage for the combined card. A maintenance man is greatly concerned with properly completing his labor card because that is often the basis for his pay. Filling out the separate work order may seem extraneous to him at this point. Combining the two functions on one card will improve the accuracy and completeness of the necessary action and material information.

Whether the cards are separate or combined, a choice between hand-written or clock-punched times must still be made. On the plus side for hand-written times is elimination of the nuisance of finding a punch clock every time another job is started. Some systems have special clocks keyed for certain departmental operations, which means the maintenance man must return to his shop when starting a new job. The advantage of the hand system would then be related to the range of workers from a clock station. If the distance is great and job changes are frequent, the hand system is best.

Another positive aspect of the hand method is the space allowed on the card. It won't matter for separate labor reporting cards where there is a separate card for each period worked on a job, but several on-off punches clutter up the combined labor-work order card. The hand-written method allows just single elapsed-time entries on the card. On the combined card, which contains more information, less space can be allocated for time entries.

The principal advantage of the clock-punch method is accuracy. A maintenance man is less likely to forget to clock-punch than to write times on the card. The choice of system depends primarily on the reliability level of the men involved and the working distance from proper time clocks.

If You Want That Part on the Shelf Next Year, Make Sure You Mark It Down on That Card.

The material usage card complements the labor reporting card as the main input sources to the maintenance data collection system. Because inventory systems were one of the first applications of the computer and because most companies have some sort of stockroom inventory system, the filling out of material requisition cards is not a new experience to most maintenance men.

The following are items which must be included in the composition of the card.

1. *Item Name:* This must be both the standard name used in the plant to describe the part or material and it must correspond to its listing in the plant inventory catalog.
2. *Manufacturer's Number or Size:* This is a manufacturer's catalog number or the size of the part, if size is normally used to describe the part. There is no need to elaborate on the description of the part needed. Bear in mind what you want to see on a read-out listing labor and material used on a certain repair project. That is, we want a description that anyone would recognize in analyzing the read-out in a repeated use situation.
3. *Catalog Number:* This local code number is, when used, all the description necessary. This number initiates the more complete description drawn from a data storage file for use in a material usage report. The verbal description is used for visual reference when an item is submitted for approval by a foreman or is checked by stockroom personnel or, of course, in the event the stockroom is operated on a manually posted inventory system.
4. *Activity Designation:* This describes the activity for which the part

or material is used and varies from plant to plant depending on individual accounting systems. This field might include such titles as Account Number, Shop Order Number, Shop Repair Account Number, and Control Number.

5. *Work Order Number:* This identifies the particular job assignment.

6. *Date:* Self-explanatory.

Here's This Card Back; Let's Fill It Out Right.

Herein lies the supporting member of our whole system: Input data must be accurate or the most elaborate and sophisticated system will produce little but meaningless results. And so before discussing the fundamental operation of an EDP-oriented control system, we must consider the problem of the working man's acceptance of this method.

There are very few plants that don't have some system of assigning labor hours to jobs. The average maintenance man, therefore, is accustomed to accounting for his time by some method, such as a work record sheet or individual job cards. If this is the case, an EDP system shouldn't be difficult to sell. If not, a thorough selling job is required.

What is the psychology of the situation? What is the maintenance man's thinking about this procedure? Generally, he is not going to be exposed to the reports resulting from the system, so he is not likely to see any purpose in what, to him, is a time-consuming task of filling out the cards. If the time is his only objection, then the situation is more easily correctable than if his feelings are of suspicion and mistrust. It is not uncommon for a worker to view the procedure as a means of keeping track of him personally.

While it is possible to make the card-filling-out a part of the job and demand that it be done, this approach, most certainly, will produce errors. These errors will either be fed into the system or will require considerable time on the part of the foreman to correct them. The possibility of error due to indifference does not rest entirely with the maintenance man. The foreman, as final checker of the data input cards, must not be allowed to make only perfunctory efforts in checking them.

Sell the Operating People

We must, quite obviously, sell operating people on what the system is intended to do, and why. The foremen should attend a few familiarization meetings to learn the mechanics of the system. At these meetings, we should go into some detail about the reports generated from the system and how they will help the foreman personally in his job. When he can see the advantages of the system histories, of automatic scheduling, of cost records for machines he's known to have outlasted their usefulness, of standards which will help him pinpoint his best and/or his worst worker, of itemized vehicle costs, and backlogs which may help to get more people, he will be in a good frame of mind to help make the system operate properly.

While it is difficult to show personal advantages of the EDP system to the maintenance man, we must, at least, get him together with manageable groups and explain what the system is going to do. Avoid stressing areas of application which make the system seem like a watchdog over the maintenance man. We must concentrate on allaying any suspicions he might have. Emphasis should be on the record-keeping and scheduling aspect of the system. Persuade the man that he will be participating in a better controlled, better organized department in which it will be more enjoyable to work. Show him samples of the specific reports the system will generate and tell him generally how they will be used. Emphasize his role in basic data input. A block diagram showing him as the foundation of the system is good. Participation as an important contributing member of a professional system will give some importance to the otherwise bothersome effort to fill in the cards.

How the EDP System Actually Works

It is time, now, to select a system and show how it functions. We will use what is probably a more sophisticated system than most because it is a goal to which all, eventually, should point. A newcomer to maintenance EDP may want to use a system incorporating a little less automation in order to better bridge the gap between manual and machine operation.

Our system incorporates a combined work order-labor reporting input card, hereafter called a work order, along with a separate material usage card. Most important the material function, which is normally an administrative, accounting, or the treasurer's responsibility, is separated from the maintenance operation, which normally exists as part of the production family.

Let's first examine the operation from the standpoint of how the work order gets to the maintenance man (see Figure 3-2).

Preventive Maintenance and Pre-Scheduled Work Cards

Pre-printed cards are made up from a master schedule of all preventive maintenance requirements and other jobs which are done routinely on a scheduled basis. Examples of the latter would be sprinkler system checks or annual heating system work. Preventive maintenance and pre-scheduled work cards are printed periodically — usually weekly — and are sent to the maintenance department for dispatch by the scheduler. They are usually dated, "week of . . . ." In a large company, where there is a crew that does nothing other than preventive maintenance, it is possible for the computer to schedule all that daily work based on standard times. In most cases, however, the scheduler will have to match the inspections with manpower and machine availability during the scheduled week.

Backlog Work

There are work requests, written by production supervisors for work other than emergency breakdown types; and these jobs become part of the backlog. The work cards are printed with "work required" and "estimated time" which are noted on the original work request by the maintenance foreman or estimator. Such backlog work orders are kept by the maintenance scheduler, to be used as his schedule allows.

Call-in Work

A call-in job must be done right away. It involves work which, if not done immediately, will result in a loss of production or present a safety hazard. Depending upon the physical size and set-up of the

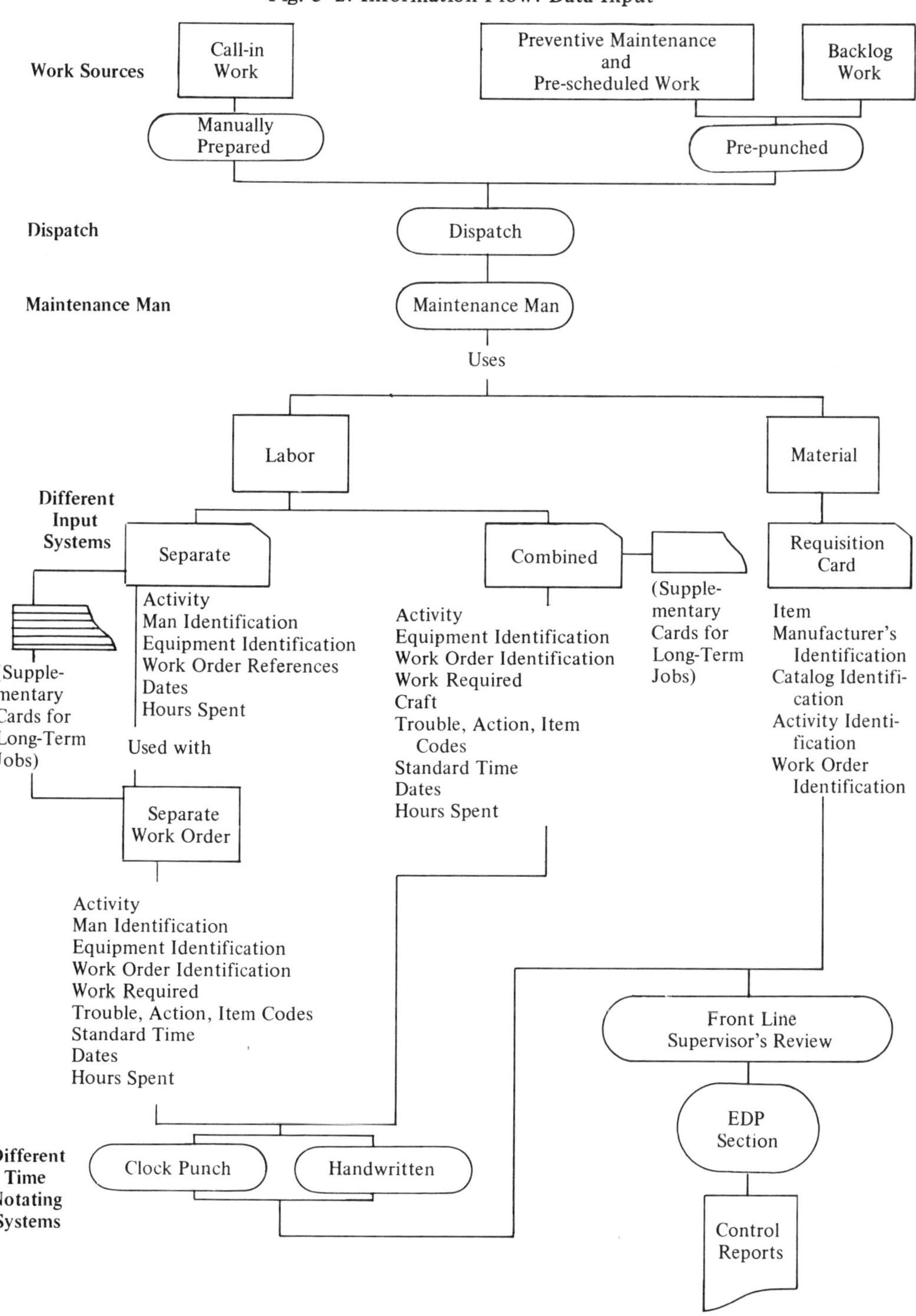

Fig. 3–2: Information Flow: Data Input

Work Sources

Call-in Work

Preventive Maintenance and Pre-scheduled Work

Backlog Work

Manually Prepared

Pre-punched

Dispatch

Dispatch

Maintenance Man

Maintenance Man

Uses

Different Input Systems

Labor

Material

Separate

Combined

Requisition Card

Activity
Man Identification
Equipment Identification
Work Order References
Dates
Hours Spent

(Supplementary Cards for Long-Term Jobs)

Activity
Equipment Identification
Work Order Identification
Work Required
Craft
Trouble, Action, Item Codes
Standard Time
Dates
Hours Spent

(Supplementary Cards for Long-Term Jobs)

Item
Manufacturer's Identification
Catalog Identification
Activity Identification
Work Order Identification

Used with

Separate Work Order

Activity
Man Identification
Equipment Identification
Work Order Identification
Work Required
Trouble, Action, Item Codes
Standard Time
Dates
Hours Spent

Front Line Supervisor's Review

EDP Section

Different Time Notating Systems

Clock Punch

Handwritten

Control Reports

plant, the maintenance scheduler (or dispatcher) will either write in the work required on a blank work order and give it to the foreman involved; or, if the trouble site and repairmen are remote, he will contact the foreman or repairman in that area and relate the problem verbally, and the foreman or repairman will then transcribe the problem on a blank card which he carries.

It is obvious that the precise procedure will vary with the plant size and crew location (such as the difference between central maintenance and area maintenance). The basic categories mentioned above hold true in any case; that is, the system requires pre-printed work cards for scheduled and backlog work, and manually-filled-in blank cards for call-in emergency work when there isn't time to process a printed card.

Communication of direction is vital to any system. The following is a sample procedural memo on work order control.

WORK ORDER CONTROL

As our work backlog grows, so does the necessity to maintain absolute, tight control over each and every work order. This procedure will refine and add to our present practice.

1. Each incoming work order must be processed completely (in the department) within one day of receipt.
2. The maintenance scheduler will initially identify the work order according to one of the following types:
    a. Emergency — work already started because of a breakdown, or work which must be done to meet a production requirement such as a spider build-up or drill rail change.
    b. Backlog — work of varying priority which is to be placed in backlog to be scheduled at a later time. Such work orders may require further scheduling of the machine or they may be able to be worked on at any time.
    c. Minor jobs — any job requiring two hours or less will be sent immediately to the foreman involved to be used as fill work. No minor jobs will be maintained in backlog. Foremen are to assign such work to fill in end of day and to prevent stretching out of jobs (i.e., assign one-hour job at noon so man knows he must complete current job *plus* the one-hour job).

3. The flow chart (Figure 3-3) summarizes the movement of our work orders from receipt to completion.
4. The following are reminders of procedures now in effect which must be followed to the letter in order to maintain smooth flow and absolute control of work orders:
   a. The primary purpose of this system is to maintain a knowledge of the status of each and every work order submitted to us. Realistically, action on some jobs will be delayed by other departments — production, engineering, purchasing, etc. These must be reviewed periodically by the scheduler and follow-up action taken on the stragglers.
   b. No work order can be allowed to remain out of position in the flow scheme. We receive about twenty work orders each day and have 200–300 in our backlog. If each work order is not handled expeditiously and placed in its proper niche, we very soon will have chaos at the scheduler's desk and at the department dispatch board.
      (1) Incoming work orders must be printed at the computer center, sorted by type, and foreman review started the same day they are received.
      (2) Foreman must review tooling and parts and note time estimate and priorities within a day of their receipt. Scheduler is to request machine time, if necessary, within a day.
      (3) Scheduled work orders, not completed, not carried over to the next day, must be returned to the scheduler before the foreman leaves that day.
      (4) Completed work is to be brought up to the scheduler, by the foremen, at the end of the day. Unexpected carry-over jobs must be brought to the scheduler's attention and the schedule rearranged before the end of the day.
      (5) *No* work order (*repeat: no work order*) is to be in the dispatch rack unless it is a job to be worked on that day.
5. The scheduler is the key to this system. He must act quickly and decisively on each and every work order. Any problems in processing work orders through maintenance foremen, production control, purchasing, etc., must be brought to the department manager's attention immediately for corrective action.
6. The bulk of our backlog has been, and will continue to be, in the general repair area. This work must be filed in order of priority (principally by date) and reviewed and updated periodically by the scheduler.
7. Parts and material ordering information is the responsibility of the foreman. The scheduler has responsibility to insure that material requests are complete before ordering and will assist the foreman, if necessary, in locating parts books, prints, and catalogs.
8. The clerk must insure that completed work orders (both copies) are

Fig. 3–3: Flow Chart

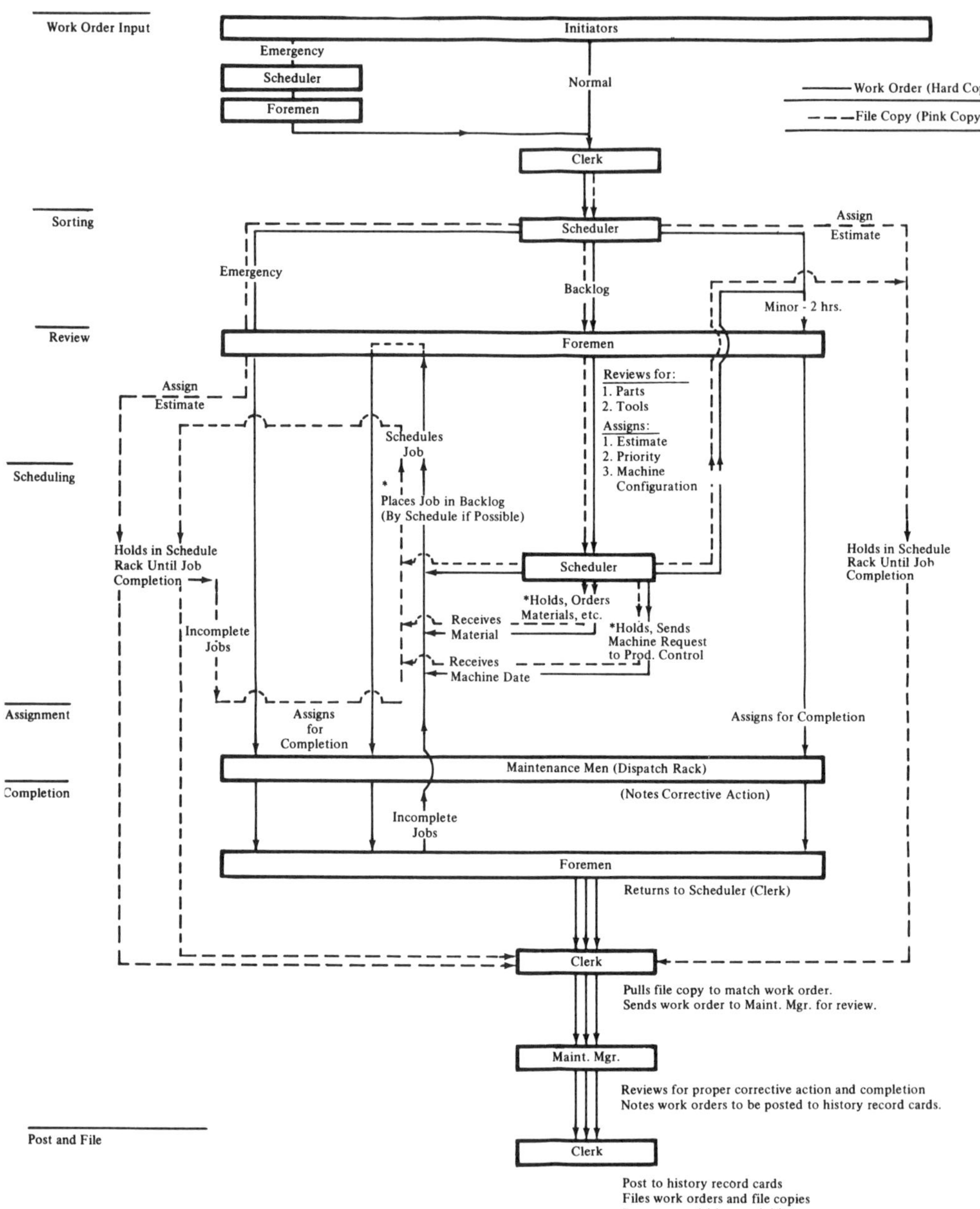

READY TO GO JOBS	JOBS IN PROGRESS (W.O's DOWN)	JOBS SCHEDULED	JOBS HELD
General Repair No. 1	To Complete Today	Week of __________, etc.	Waiting Material
General Repair No. 2	To Complete Tomorrow	Vacation, 19__________	Waiting Engineering
General Repair No. 3	Minor Jobs	Saturday Work	Waiting Production
Machine Repair	Awaiting Proper Mach. Conditions	Sunday Work	Waiting Machine Schedule
Plumbing-Heating		Outside Contractors	Date (Prod. Control)
Carpentry-Bldg. Repair			Waiting Schedule Arrangements
Electrical No. 1			(Maint. Scheduler)
Electrical No. 2			
Electrical No. 3			
Machining			

pulled from the rack and filed. It will be her responsibility to insure that work orders are returned for all file copies in the "Work to be Completed Today" file, even to the extent of personally questioning the foremen as to their whereabouts.

The prime consideration for success of our system is "Today's Work Today." A foreman or scheduler should not leave for the day unless that day's incoming and completed work has been properly processed. Carryovers are cumulative and do nothing but snarl the system. We cannot operate without the system, so it is the responsibility of each of us to make the system work for and not against us.

Maintenance Man's Function

The maintenance man punches or writes in his starting time and finishing time for the job as he moves from one assignment to another. He also adds his name and clock number. On call-in work directed to him, he also notes the machine or account number and makes some notation of the work required. After the job is completed, he notes the work required and corrective action code on the card. This man is responsible for making sure the total time on that day's work cards equals the time he spent working (normally, eight hours). If a task presumes a skill level higher than is available, the checking operation is handled by the time-keeping function.

The greatest problem arises in jobs which carry over for several days and involve a number of people. To elaborate, the EDP control system is ideal for a job started and completed in one day, and with no more men required for the job than there are spaces for names. Because there are carry-over jobs and because there are several men on some jobs, there must be supplementary cards. These blank cards are filled in by the maintenance men, who copy pertinent information from the original or master card.

In most cases, it is obvious when a job will require more than one day's work. The foreman or scheduler then must line through the "hour reporting" portion of the card or make a similar notation that this card is to remain in the schedule rack and that labor times are to be reported on supplemental cards. Similarly, when the "name" blanks are filled in on a given job, it is obvious to any additional men working on that job that they will have to fill out a supplemental card. We can, therefore, envision a situation where an "original" card is in the schedule rack for several days and men are filling out supplemental cards each day for time spent on that job.

The supplementary cards are completely void of any pre-printing; that is, they do not have a work order number. The information which must be transcribed from the original to the supplemental card includes a work order number, with name, clock number, craft code, and hours worked. The work order number keys the supplementary to the original card. The original is turned in when the job is completed and carries all essential data, such as work required and code, corrective action code, machine or account number, etc. It may be necessary to close out an open job at the end of a reporting period for the purpose of report completeness. The original can be returned from the accounting function or a duplicate initialed.

Input Card Review

We now have our tradesmen working with three different work card situations.

1. *Initial (pre-printed)*: This has the job information pre-printed and is either a scheduled inspection or a backlog work order. Because it is initial, it has a pre-printed work order number.
2. *Initial (non-printed)*: This is a blank to be used for emergency call-in work. Because it, too, is initial, it has a pre-printed work order number.
3. *Supplementary (non-printed)*: These cards are completely blank. They are used to supplement a master card when a job is extended beyond its initial day and when more men are involved than there is space to list on the card.

The card system lends itself well to a schedule rack type of dispatching system in which each maintenance man has his own pocket or slot where the foreman can place work cards according to the way he wants the work assigned. Where more than one man is assigned to a job, a note can be placed in the additional man's slot stating: "W.O. 56832 w/D. Smith."

The material usage card is simply a record of every piece of material and spare part used. It is used in the inventory control system, whether manually posted or computerized, and furnishes material cost information. The critical data on this card is the work order number and the machine, or account, number. The item cost is generally added in the accounting function in a manual system and listed on the inventory run in a comupterized system. The information from the material usage card is used to complete some of the machine and job cost reports.

We have discussed the types of input cards used, the origin of these cards, and how and under which circumstances the cards are filled out. The following sections elaborate on the many uses for the input data but, so that we can have a general feeling for the applications at the outset, we will discuss them briefly now.

Preview of Applications

There is really no end to the different kinds of reports possible from basic maintenance data. The up-to-date maintenance manager develops a feeling or state of mind in which weighing computer research and reports is the first step in solving many problems. And, once he has gained a thorough knowledge of the data available, taking that first step is automatic.

Basically, we are looking for better control. The EDP reports generated describe in any detail desired the work that is to be done and, later, how long the work took and what it cost.

An intrinsic advantage of a controlled system is the placing of planning responsibility right into the hands of the front line supervisor. The following *job preparation* format explains the steps to be followed by the foreman when reviewing each work order.

JOB PREPARATION

We have made great strides toward increasing the percentage of *scheduled* maintenance work. Our preparation for this scheduled work must complement this effort. To assist us in job preparation, the following procedure will be used.

Immediately upon obtaining a scheduled date for a job, scheduler will note the date on the work order and send this work order to the foreman involved. He will also send, for review, all other work orders which do not require immediate work and which will be placed in our backlog.

The foreman will review the job requirements to determine the following:

1. Parts
2. Materials
3. Tools

He will order any of the above that are needed.

When he is satisfied that all necessary parts and materials are on hand or ordered, he will initial the work order in the material block and return it to the scheduler. To minimize "job start" time, all special tools, parts, and materials for a scheduled job will be stored together in the maintenance shop as they are received.

Job requirements will be discussed on the afternoon prior to the job with the maintenance men involved. The otherwise "wasted" last few minutes of the day are to be spent readying for the next day's job.

Through this procedure, we should tend to eliminate last-minute bearing orders, numerous trips to suppliers, and time spent searching for tools and waiting in the stockroom for materials while a machine is down.

The basic work reports should deal in labor hours spent, including time spent in repair, in preventive maintenance, in miscellaneous accounts, in new construction, or any other definable area. The reports show man-hours and costs against individual machines, and, when repair codes are used, labor hours accumulated for each type of repair. Standards can be evaluated and individual exceptions, good and bad, highlighted. A report with any combination of men and machines can be derived from these data.

Data Storage

Any system planner will soon learn the hard, cold facts of life: that his *total system* must account for a practical limit in storage capacity for his many bits of information. There is a definite limit, both economically and physically, when, for example, a maintenance system must share with all the other production and accounting systems in an organization.

Disc packs and tapes have greatly increased storage capacities, but there are financial limits here, too. We must consider, also, the practical limitation to the cataloging and organizational effort required in any size data processing center.

The total system presented in this book requires considerable storage space, but not necessarily a great deal of memory space. Both for simplicity in understanding and for practical purposes, the data inputs and most reference data are set up on punch cards and subsequent decks thereof. The individual data processing group would have to determine which information to maintain in card packs and which information to convert to memory discs.

Each of the following chapters will deal with a specific application of maintenance data.

IV. Cost Control

Cost control is the first application considered because it is of prime importance to the maintenance manager, and it is an area where we can realize a great profit-saving benefit.

Labor Cost Reports

Every maintenance labor hour — where it was spent and how much cost was accrued — is detailed in the labor cost report. Since we are primarily concerned with identifying problem areas, we should show the hours and dollars against each machine. The same figures can be used in the equipment cost record. The following is a suggested breakdown of how the labor hours can be reported. This report should be issued monthly (see Figure 4-1).

Repair Report by Machine, by Work Order Number

This report lists, in numerical order, each machine on which work is performed and the hours and cost of each work order. A total will be shown for each machine.

Preventive Maintenance Report by Machine

This is a listing, in numerical order of each machine, preventive work performed and its hours and cost.

New Installation Project Report

This lists each project by shop order or other identifying designation with the hours and cost of each.

Fig. 4-1: Format of Labor and Material Cost Report

Equipment Identification	Work Order	Labor Hours	Labor Cost	Material Cost	Total Cost	
1003	57863	3.2	$ 20.42	$ —	$ 20.42	
1003	57902	12.1	81.63	629.00	710.63	
1003	57941	1.7	11.88	11.42	23.30	
					764.35*	
1003	P.M.	3.8	23.90	—	23.90*	
Etc.	—	—	—	—		$39,837.52
New Installation Projects						
10763	56982	48.0	$ 288.00	$ 490.00	$ 778.00	
					2263.44*	
11002	57881	32.8	198.42	206.10	404.52	
—	—	—	—	—	404.52*	
—	—	—	—	—	—	
Etc.	—	—	—	—	—	$ 9,368.40
Miscellaneous Accounts						
Plant Protection		720	3676.00	—	3676.00*	
Custodians		480	2472.00	—	2472.00*	
Maintenance Supplies		—	—	3227.60	—	
Etc.		—	—	—		$11,298.36
		10040	50202.16	10302.12		$60,504.28

*Subtotal

Miscellaneous Accounts Report

This list gives the hours and dollars spent on accounts specified for items like plant protection personnel, custodial personnel, power house personnel, lubrication personnel, and the many not otherwise defined accounts for work that must be performed in and around an industrial plant.

Special Work Areas Where It Is Desirable to Monitor Costs

Such reports differ from the account category above since for some jobs we may want a further breakdown by machine or other designation. An example would be some routine task, such as a machine set-up charge, where we want to know how many hours are involved and in what area or on which machines the work is being performed.

Material Cost Reports

Repairs, by Machine, by Work Order Number

The material cost information is best reported on the same printout as the machine work order labor hour report (see Figure 4-1). A third column on that form shows total cost (labor and material) for that particular work order.

Preventive Maintenance by Machine

This information can also be added to the machine (preventive maintenance) labor hour report. There normally won't be much material used on the inspections, but what there is must be accounted for.

By New Installation Project, by Miscellaneous Account, by Special Work Areas

Again, material costs can be added to the respective labor hour report as an additional column. A total column is used to show total expenditure for that particular project, account, or special work area.

By Maintenance Supplies

There are maintenance materials used, such as oil, grease, cleaning supplies, etc., which aren't assigned to a particular work order or project but still amount to a considerable sum and, in any case, must be considered in the total maintenance cost picture. These costs can be listed in columns with verbal identification replacing the numerical designations used in the other material reports.

These material reports include costs from outside vendors, from stockroom inventory, and from outside vendors to replenish stockroom inventory. Because the source of this data is explicit — material usage cards for stockroom items and completed purchase orders or receiving slips for outside vendors — it is possible to key this difference into the report. The easiest way is to show on this report the purchase order number on each item used directly from an outside vendor.

This method is an advantage to the person ordering an item at a future date. While purchasing maintains a standard cost on oft-ordered items, the seldom-ordered items often incur the greatest cost. Rather than sorting through the accounting or purchasing copies of old purchase orders, the purchaser can check the material report for the month (or month after) when that order was received, find the cost listed under the machine or project number, and identify it by the purchase order number.

It may also be advantageous for some key purchases (over a certain dollar amount) to be posted to the maintenance copy of the purchase order as soon as the material reports are received each month. Any advantage to this procedure would be negated if quotes are required for every purchase, and the cost information is already with the purchase order.

Working Cost Control Reports

The cost control reports, both labor and material, described above, are primarily historical in nature. While their detail is absolutely necessary for specific analysis, we also need a less detailed, more categorical report through which the maintenance manager can identify problem areas and unfavorable trends.

Of considerable importance, then, is the system developed to identify the categories to be analyzed. The main categories should be machine numbers and general account numbers, mentioned previously. These are a part of an established accounting procedure in every plant and will not be initiated solely for the maintenance computer program. However, the important point is that, with our program, we can establish additional areas of identification, assign code numbers according to a logical plan, and then proceed to analyze cost data from any combination of identifiable areas desired.

Remember, though, that these codes are entered on the input data cards by humans and so are subject to error and confusion. Activity identification must, therefore, not be so complex as to cause error and defeat its original purpose.

In addition to machine numbers and general account numbers, it may be desirable to evaluate results by type of production activity.

Other possible categories would be physical areas or even managerial areas. The first digit in the machine or account number is commonly used to identify plant or production area.

Following is an example of the type of information on a summary report which will identify problem areas.

**EXAMPLE OF TYPE OF INFORMATION ON A SUMMARY REPORT
TO IDENTIFY PROBLEM AREAS**

LABOR ($)

	Production Areas	Total
Repair		
Preventive Maintenance		
Installation Projects		
Miscellaneous Account		
(Any Special Work Areas)		
Plant Protection		
Custodial		
Power House		
Lubrication		

MATERIAL ($)

Machine Repair		
Preventive Maintenance		
Installation Projects		
Miscellaneous Accounts		
Maintenance Supplies		
Lubrication		
(Any Special Areas)		
Total Labor & Material		

Historical Costs

Before any form of investment theory can be applied, the maintenance manager must have accurate maintenance cost records. Some plants do not maintain accurate records; others have cumbersome, manually posted account books. It is a logical step from the monthly labor and material reports to a report showing annual costs and total cumulative costs for any piece of equipment or any area of maintenance.

While this report is furnished annually for historical purposes, an interim monthly report, showing trends, is also necessary. For example, year-end total cost observed in January might be well in line with past history but, if costs start to accelerate in the first part of the year, we don't want to have to wait until the end of the year to discover this fact.

We will call this interim report the trend report. It should list each machine and maintenance area by its identifying number and then list opposite each item that month's total material and labor costs. The next cost columns serve as references and show the total cost for each item for the past six months, or previous year-to-date, or average over last two years, or whatever reference is most meaningful for the plant's operation.

It is entirely within the capability of the computer to calculate an average of past costs, applying a given tolerance such as plus 10%, and print out the percentage increase opposite each machine number. This figure serves to flag those items which should be more fully investigated.

The most complete trend report will take the form shown in Figure 4-2. With this form, the maintenance manager can scan quickly the percent increase column and, for any one that shows an unusual jump, he can check the past six months' column to see if this was just an exceptional month or whether it is part of a developing trend of increased costs for this maintenance area.

While the monthly trend report is designed to identify short-term cost increases, it does not necessarily show long-term gradual increases. This area of maintenance cost control is covered by the year end (trend) report. This approach is incorporated into the annual cost report (see Figure 4-3). This report also incorporates a total accumulated labor and material cost. The method of analysis is identical to that used on the monthly reports.

Follow-up action when a trouble area is spotted involves checking

Fig. 4–2: General Format of Monthly (Trend) Report

Activity (Machine) Number	Monthly Labor & Material Cost	Monthly Average of Previous Year's To Date Labor & Material Cost	% Increase This Month Over Previous Monthly Average	Past Six Months Total Labor & Material Cost					

Fig. 4–3: General Format of Annual Cost (Trend) Report

Activity (Machine) Number	Annual Labor & Material Cost	Total Accumulated Labor & Material Cost	Annual Average of Previous Year's Labor & Material Cost	% Increase This Year Over Previous Annual Average	Past Five Years Total Labor & Material Cost				

the detailed labor cost report and the material cost report to determine where the increase is occurring.

Investment Planning

This cost information leads us to investment planning. While this subject, whether utilizing Present Value, Average Investment, Machinery and Allied Products Institute (M.A.P.I.), or another method, is a complex field by itself, we should mention the adaptability of these analyses to the computer method. The information required in these methods includes investment cost, depreciation and salvage value, all of which can be assigned to each machine on a one-time basis subject to periodic review. Maintenance costs are derived from our annual cost (trend) report. Operating cost can be taken from production reports and also assigned on a one-time basis subject to periodic review.

We can visualize now a program set-up which can be used periodically to check the replacement position of a machine or group of machines. We can derive a present value or other investment criteria to be compared to another alternative, such as a replacement machine. These programs will produce results which reflect up-to-date maintenance costs.

Figure 4-4 shows one format for a work paper used to set up the equipment replacement review program. A card is punched with this information for each piece of equipment to be considered for review. There should be some selectivity to avoid a burdensome report. Equipment selected should be that of shorter depreciation schedule, with high maintenance costs, or that which is to be compared to a more productive piece of machinery.

When this information is incorporated on a series of punch cards, a report can be generated on a periodic (usually annual) basis or for review during a capital improvement study. The report usually has the same format as Figure 4-5.

At times of periodic review, the old report is re-run (if the old print-out is not to be found), and this becomes the work sheet. All items are reviewed and changed on the report. Of particular note are

Fig. 4-4: Format for Work Paper (and Report) for
Equipment Replacement Review Program (Average Investment Method)

Equipment Identification	Original Cost	Years to Salvage (Age)	Salvage Value	Average Annual Maintenance Cost	Operating Cost	Interest	Total Annual Cost

(Two arrays for each piece of equipment; one for present, one for proposed replacement)

Fig. 4–5: Information Flow: Cost Control Reports

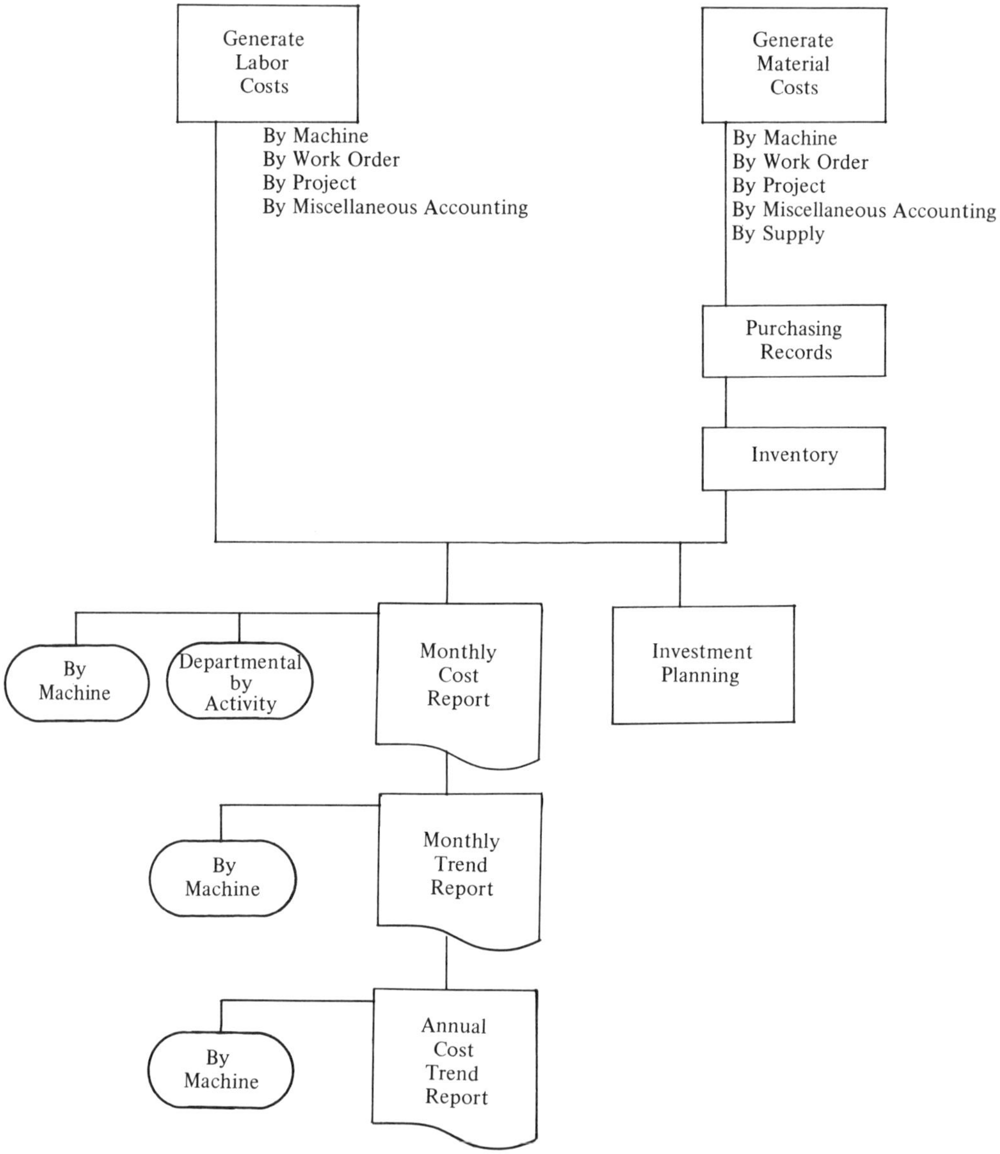

current interest rates, new production figures, costs of newer machines, and, of course, up-to-date maintenance costs. The latter maintenance costs can be selected by the computer from the cards or memory supplying cost information for the trend reports, and automatically updated. Other pertinent information changes mentioned above must be added by hand and new cards punched. A new report then follows.

Average Investment Theory

To make the foregoing more meaningful and to help the maintenance manager direct the data processing people on how to set up the program, we will deviate momentarily to discuss the theory involved in investment planing. We have chosen average annual investment because it is a basic system and easily understood by the novice in investment theory. (For the exponents of present value theory, the present value factor tables and the equations involved can easily be assimilated by the computer. Our basic work paper will provide the necessary information.)

The average investment method estimates the average cost of owning, operating, and maintaining a piece of equipment. This cost is compared to the costs of alternatives.

The following describes the segments of average cost which are added for a final comparable total.

1. Average Annual Salvage Loss (New Cost − Salvage Value/Year to Salvage): This accounts for the loss in actual value for each year owned, assuming a straight line value decline.
2. Annual Interest on Investment (Interest Rate × (New Cost + Salvage Value)/2): Accounts for interest demanded by money otherwise spent on the investment.
3. Average Annual Maintenance Costs: Total labor and material over past few years or anticipated costs for newly considered replacement.
4. Average Annual Operating Costs: Includes labor and property taxes which vary for each alternative.

It is important that a common productive output base be used for each alternative. Either adjust costs per unit of product or apply a factor reflecting the ratio of productive output.

In summation, we see our labor and material cost information being used in several directions of control: to build historical maintenance cost figures for each piece of equipment to determine its current replacement position; to show in which type of work maintenance hours are being spent; to show operating costs on a monthly basis which indicates overall departmental effectiveness and which can be used in budget forecasting; to derive itemized trend reports which point out recent high cost offenders; to obtain purchase price history to be used in reordering; and, to make countless combinations of these.

V. Scheduling and Preventive Maintenance

Scheduling of Maintenance Work

We have discussed three categories of maintenance jobs in relation to the types of data cards used: (1) preventive maintenance and pre-scheduled work; (2) backlog work; and, (3) call-in work.

The uncertain nature of a maintenance department's operation makes it unrealistic to attempt daily computer scheduling of backlog work beyond priority listing on a backlog report. Besides the fact that breakdowns can seriously disrupt a department's scheduled work (particularly a small department), there are too many personal and immediate arrangements which must be made between production schedulers and maintenance schedulers. Conditions of machine availability, manpower availability, and rush production requirements change hourly and, while the computer could easily digest the information and rearrange schedules, the schedulers involved can make the arrangements necessary and have the work on the way by the time the decisions and conditions are transferred to the computer and a report received.

Scheduling of work within the shop has been avoided because this writer believes that data processing equipment can add very little to the efficiency of the shop planners, supervisors, and schedulers.[1]

1. A. V. Paletti, "Data Processing Equipment in Evaluating Maintenance Operations," *Techniques of Plant Engineering and Maintenance,* Vol. XV (New York: Clapp and Poliak, 1964), p. 72.

The computer can best help us, then, in the areas of pre-scheduled work and preventive maintenance. We will treat each of these separately.

Pre-scheduled or Block Projects

The type of work involved here may be defined as predictable work of some repair, cleaning, or checking nature not necessarily in the category of preventive maintenance.

Examples of such *pre-scheduled work* are: (a) "Close and seal upper bay windows for winter"; (b) "Clean and start cooling tower operation"; (c) "Collect transformer oil samples"; (d) "Check fuel oil supply."

Examples of *block projects* are: (a) "painting" each plant area, scheduled over a period of years; (b) "roof repair," each plant roof coating scheduled over a period of years; (c) "major overhauls"; (d) "standardized equipment installations."

Please bear in mind we are seeking improved control. The ability of EDP to assist us will depend largely on the scope, or simply the number, of the jobs that we must insure will be completed. If these are few in number, a simple one-page check list on the maintenance manager's desk will suffice. However, most plants have a great number of these miscellaneous maintenance-type tasks which must be accomplished seasonally, annually, or on some other time basis. Unless they are scheduled, we must rely on someone to remember to do them, and this latter system is anything but infallible. Much pre-scheduled work is minor in nature, but can be annoying to personnel if it is not done on time.

We recall our earlier discussion of maintenance department image. The more jobs that we can do without having specific requests from production people, the better impression we can make. A printed schedule with a follow-up delinquency report can assist us in keeping our plants in top operating condition.

Pre-Scheduled Work

Setting up a *pre-scheduled work* schedule means listing every job that can be so controlled. This may mean reviewing old work orders and conducting a brainstorming session with department supervisors. Next, a standard time is assigned to each job, along with the approximate date each job is to be done. The computer will balance the workload and publish a monthly (or whatever frequency is desired) schedule that lists which jobs are to be done in each week. If the department is large enough to assign men full time to this type of work, the schedule will be for each day.

A periodic delinquency report, listing jobs not completed, is included as part of the basic work schedule (see Figure 5-1).

Fig. 5-1: Format for Pre-Scheduled Work Schedule

Month of: May

Equipment Building Description	*Work Required*	*Work Order Number*	*Week of:* 1 2 3 4
Building 7	Open seal, upper bay windows	56241	past due
Building 6B	Clean; start cooling tower	58733	X
General Plant	Collect transformer oil samples	58734	X
Power House	Check fuel oil supply	58755	X
Parking lots	Re-stripe park lots	58764	X X

Block Projects

Block projects are only slightly different from pre-scheduled work in nature in that they form one specific job involving many phases rather than the previously discussed series of many small jobs. For such items as painting and roof repair, costs are assigned to each plant area (which can be building, section, bay, etc.), along with the frequency for the job (e.g., every four years). The computer accounts for these factors and prints out a balanced cost schedule of which area is to be worked on during each year. It is possible, for example, to include in this cost balancing procedure a requirement for certain adjacent roofs to be worked on at the same time (see Figure 5-2).

This schedule can be extended indefinitely but, normally, a projection of ten years is realistic, due to changing methods and materials which affect job frequency requirements. An annual inspection tour of roofs and painted areas will confirm or negate the current schedule. Now the computer comes into its own. The inspection will, undoubtedly, reveal acceleration or postponement of work scheduled for that year or the next. This information can be returned to the computer and it will print a new schedule based on these adjusted requirements. While a scheduler could fight through an initial schedule and justify the time spent over a period of years, it is these annual adjustments that bring the computer to the front.

Major overhauls and equipment moving can be adapted to computer scheduling only if they occur often enough to have established times for each segment of the job. The next step is to assign restrictions to each job element such as "must precede element 31, but occur after element 24," or, "cannot be done at same time as element 19." By furnishing the available man-hours available for each period, the manager will receive a schedule with all elements arranged in the most efficient order.

It may seem that a lot of preparatory work is required to achieve a schedule that a scheduler could also devise; it does. But, consider the changes in plans that will take place, such as eliminating or adding an element, or increasing or decreasing the time for an element. Once a program is written for a project, it is a simple step to change or add elements and have a new schedule printed. EDP personnel will simply pull the card for the element to be changed, punch another card reflecting the change in restriction, and process a new schedule.

Work Orders

A corollary to computer scheduling is, of course, the printing of work orders for items on the schedule. It is through these numbered work orders for each job (or element of a project) that a delinquency or status report can be furnished. This is accomplished by the com-

Fig. 5–2: General Format for Block Scheduling of Roof Repair, Painting, Etc.

Roof Repair

Block Description	*Work Required**	*Frequency*	*1969*	*1970*	*1971*	*1972*	*1973*	*1974*
1	1	4	—	700	—	—	—	—
2	1	4	1200	—	—	—	1200	—
3	1	5	800	—	—	—	—	800
3A	2	10	—	3000	—	—	—	—
4A	1	4	—	—	800	—	—	—
7	1	4	600	—	—	—	600	—
7	2	10	4000	—	—	—	—	—
7	3	3	500	—	—	500	—	—
etc.	—	—	—	—	—	—	—	—
			12800	14300	11900	15000	12200	13100

*Codes describe various treatments: (1) coat glass system
(2) install glass system
(3) replace felts

puter by simply comparing completed work orders to those originally issued and printing out an exception report. This type of report, usually, is necessary only on very large projects and might be required by higher management. A maintenance manager, normally, will be aware of project status on a daily basis and such a report is extraneous to his needs. (A report on the status of pre-scheduled work falls in the realm of backlog and will be discussed in Chapter X.)

Scheduling Preparation

We should pause at this time to consider the elements which must be considered in setting up a general program for cost-balancing scheduling. This procedure, and the program required, are good only when there are numerous costs to be balanced.

Any medium-sized plant has sufficient "painting segments" and "roof areas" to justify initiation of this management tool. A very small plant or institution is better advised to balance out costs manually.

The data processing people in the company will, of course, provide the final details of program requirements, but the maintenance manager should be prepared with the following information.

1. Estimated cost of each segment: This can be based on past work done or, preferably, on current quotation.
2. Time interval between work required on each segment.
3. Priority of starting times for each segment (i.e., which ones must be done first, second, etc.).
4. Allowable limits on:
   a. total dollars spent in any one year;
   b. tolerance for balanced dollars in any one year (i.e., how much excess is allowed over target amount stated in a.);
   c. how many years any one frequency can be lengthened or shortened (i.e., a roof scheduled for coating every six years might be allowed minus one, plus two years, or five to eight years).

These examples of limits are straightforward, and the principle of multiple selection which requires the limits is basic to any computerized schedule. It is easy to project this reasoning to other scheduling situations, such as lubrication, preventive maintenance, and pre-scheduled work. Examples of limits which the maintenance manager should be prepared to furnish the programmer are:

1. estimated time for each element of work to be scheduled
2. whether a job can be interrupted, and for what length of time
3. total man hours to be allotted for this type of work in any one day
4. production downtime restrictions, such as: "No more than two 8000 serial number presses down at any one time"; some equipment, coded: "Third shift maintenance only"

At this point, the reader may feel swamped with the magnitude of preparatory work required for instituting some of these programs. Bear in mind that these programs are initiated gradually, and a maintenance manager is advised to insure that each program is installed well and *used* before going on to the next one. (Reference: Case Study III, "Too Many Reports.")

Preventive Maintenance

Preventive maintenance, as a subject, has received more attention from writers than any other maintenance topic in recent years. Before detailing the application of a computer to this area, we should use this opportunity to examine preventive maintenance as a philosophy rather than as a cut-and-dried, one-two-three procedure.

Preventive Maintenance Philosophy

We are not talking about a procedure but, rather, a way of life. The change to this way of life is difficult and slow, and short-term results are insignificant. Long-term results are dramatic, but only if the metamorphosis is complete. This writer has experienced the frustrating results achieved at midpoint in the change and, also, experienced the satisfying rewards at break-through.

Too much emphasis has been placed on corrective maintenance and upon preventive maintenance only as an inspection procedure.

While this book is selling the use of the computer in maintenance, and preventive maintenance is a big part of the maintenance computer, we must emphasize preventive maintenance as a total approach and not as a mechanical system. If preventive maintenance is not faced in this manner, it will likely fail, and preventive maintenance (and the associated computer) will be written off as a nice theoretical idea.

Recent writings have indicated considerable top management interest in maintenance savings. This interest has developed partly because it is the last place to save money and partly because significant results have been attained. Many companies have become highly sophisticated in their approach to maintenance and have achieved eye-opening savings. Others have tried preventive maintenance on a halfway scale and failed, or have never tried it and are still living on a "put out the fire; what's going to happen today?" basis. It is to these latter people that this section is directed.

When a maintenance manager arrives at the plant not dreading the report of what broke down last night or what will break down today, he really feels the impact of the success of his program. This feeling reflects all the intangible benefits not directly shown in maintenance cost and downtime reports which will have already indicated success.

Beyond the inspection procedure, this maintenance manager will have had to sell, preach, and hammer his preventive philosophy into his men, his peers, and his superiors. He must have gained full top management support; without it, he might just as well have concentrated on fire fighting.

He must have stood up for his preventive maintenance schedule in the face of production's frantic request to put it off until next time. He must have influenced plant engineering to think preventive maintenance rather than strict immediate economy. He must have followed up and hammered at his own foremen and people at every opportunity to "not just get by, but repair it so it will not break again, even if it takes longer and production is screaming for the machine."

He must have followed every inspection to insure reported work was done, even at the temporary expense of other work. The maintenance man conducting an inspection must see results of his work. If he sees the same fault uncorrected on successive inspections, his interest is non-retrievable. He must insist that his foremen take time to go over every inspection with the man at the machine until he is satisfied that the inspection is complete.

He must generate an attitude of preventive maintenance, primarily with his own maintenance people but, also, with production employees and supervisors, so that all continually think of ways to prevent future breakdowns and are always on the watch for indications of potential breakdowns. He must insure that reported suggestions and problems are followed up immediately in order to sustain this interest.

This is not easy. It requires real determination and singleness of purpose to sell this program without overselling. From our experience and the apparent success of others, this period of salesmanship will take two to three years on the average.

On the reverse side of the ledger, we must be careful not to over-inspect. Inspection intervals should be reviewed annually by going over the trend reports and the inspection reports for individual machines. If a machine shows no problems, and if the men are not turning up trouble spots on the inspection, then the interval should be increased. Ideally, a proper interval eliminates all downtime except for external damage and a machine should have a few items that need correcting on at least every other inspection.

Installing a Preventive Maintenance Program

The first step is to select the machines that represent the largest downtime risk. These are the units that would cause the most disruption to production should they fail. A second selection criterion is the historical maintenance cost of the equipment. A machine with very little past trouble that is not particularly vital in the production scheme would certainly not be selected for the preventive maintenance program.

When the machines are selected, the next step is to assign inspection intervals. This, as mentioned in the previous section, is based on history and criticality. And, again, remember not to overinspect.

The largest task in setting up preventive maintenance, and perhaps the most vital to the success of the program, is writing of check lists. Ample time should be allowed for this job. The best way to write the list is to research old work orders and note the items occurring most frequently. These lists should be reviewed by the maintenance foreman most familiar with the equipment. This is a good time to start selling preventive maintenance by bringing in some of the key maintenance men and getting their opinions of items to be included in the check list.

Fig. 5–3: Information Flow: Scheduling and Preventive Maintenance

Generated By:

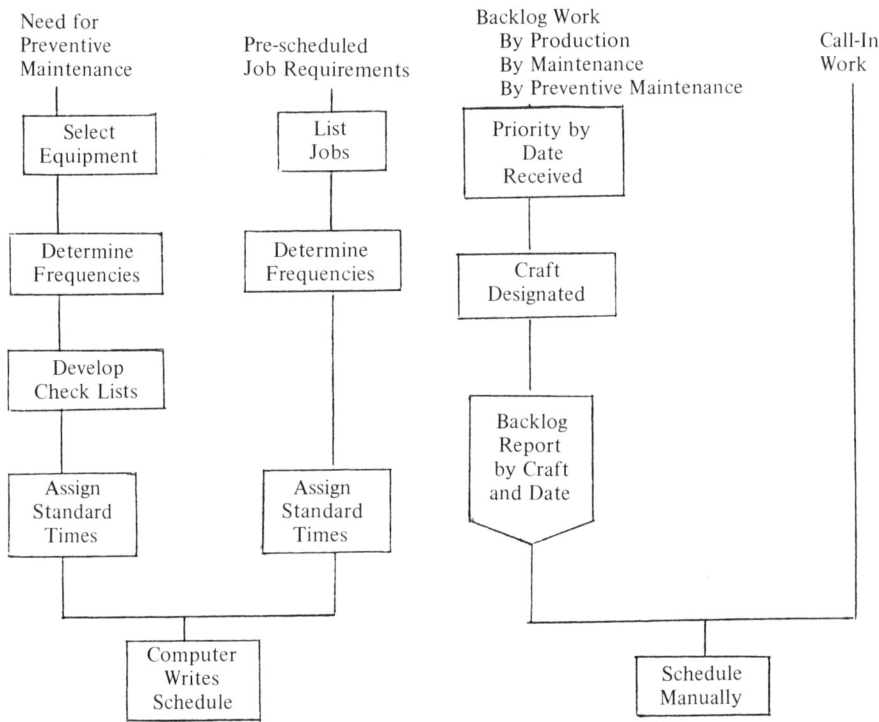

Standard times will be assigned to the inspections but, probably, not until after a few of them have been completed. These times will vary from one inspection to another because of the amount of work involved. For example, a large lathe with electronic controls will require an electrical inspection every three months, but the motors will be lubed and meggered only once every six months or annually. A standard time will have to be assigned, therefore, to each element of the inspection.

When the lists are complete, EDP will punch a card for each major element or group of small elements on the check list. This card will include, in addition to equipment identification, the inspection interval, standard time, and craft involved. We will then have a deck of cards comprising the inspection for each machine. It is then possible for the computer to develop a balanced schedule for the entire year.

If there is some restriction as to the number of machines that can be down in one area, this restriction must be coded into each machine deck so the computer can consider it when balancing the schedule. The computer will then publish a schedule which can be distributed to all production and production scheduling personnel concerned as well as to maintenance people.

The computer prints the inspection cards each week for the next week's inspection. The work cards are separated according to the craft involved; however, there may be individual cards for major items and items that are not done on each inspection. For example, all of the electrical items are printed on one card and all of the plumbing items on one card. Craft classification depends, too, on the number of items involved for each craft and the space on the card for work required.

It is obvious that there are multiple cards for some crafts on some inspections. All cards for one inspection, however, have the same printed work order number. They also have the preventive maintenance work required code pre-printed. The scheduler receives these inspection decks and distributes them by craft in exactly the same manner as for any other scheduled job.

When the maintenance men complete an inspection, they mark

"O.K." for each item on the card, or they note that work still has to be accomplished. After these cards are processed back through EDP for the collection of labor times and to close out the job, those with work required are returned to the foreman, who writes the necessary work orders. These cards are usually filed and can be run on a special report which shows the number of discrepancies found and is used when reviewing inspection intervals.

An alternate method of scheduling preventive maintenance omits printing work order cards. A single work order card is printed for the entire inspection. There are printed check lists on file in the maintenance scheduler's office which are sent along with the work order. While this system appears to be simpler, it requires a clerk to review the check lists and, from a coded schedule, to omit or add the special items which are not done every inspection.

The only argument for this method is that it works well as an interim system while maintenance men and foremen become used to working with the numerous work order cards involved in an inspection. To show, by comparison, the degree of sophistication attained recently, one original preventive maintenance method still in use has the man sent to a machine where there is a printed list of instructions for the inspections. This is, of course, undesirable from the standpoint of lack of detail in special items scheduled, and problems in transmitting work required.

CASE STUDY IV: "THE OLD SYSTEM HAS WORKED UP TO NOW."

Rathman Industries is a medium-sized firm, combining a brass foundry and a fitting processing plant. Ray Derrick had been with the company for about six months, having been assigned to understudy the retiring maintenance manager, Val Salerno.

In preparation for his soon-to-be assumed position, Ray did a lot of home study on maintenance organization and, in particular, on preventive maintenance. His study, along with his production management experience with equipment downtime, convinced him of the need for an "all stops out" maintenance program.

Confounding his theory was the existing preventive maintenance program at Rathman. It was a bona fide system, with check list and schedules. And it was ineffectual. Labor and material cost reports showed many hours spent on preventive maintenance, with an increase in repair hours. Downtime was also on the rise.

Discussion with Salerno didn't produce a direct answer to his problems. Val's comment was that the same system had been in use for some time, and he didn't know what was wrong. This gave Ray a clue to the solution. It was the *same* system, with probably no updating or revisions.

The rest of that day, Ray outlined the parts of the preventive maintenance program which had to be reviewed.

1. Schedules: How contrived, and how often reviewed?
2. Equipment selected: By what criteria?
3. Check lists: Specific and reflecting current problems.
4. Inspection method: Are we getting a thorough inspection?
5. Work-generated follow-up: Is reported work being given some priority for completion?

The majority of the next day was spent in meetings with the maintenance superintendent, the various maintenance foremen and the maintenance scheduler. All were convinced of the purpose and need for a preventive maintenance program but, having grown up with the system in use didn't see where it had lost its impact. Of particular importance were reflections by some of the foremen, to the effect: "We're just going through the motions. . . ." One reported having to correct his men repeatedly for coming back from the inspection, taking the check list from the work order rack and proceeding to run down the list with rapid check marks in the "O.K." column.

With this background, and with Val Salerno's blessing, Ray proceeded to explore in depth each item on his review list.

Schedules Selection. Frequency of inspections had changed little from the original program. An annual meeting with maintenance foremen, in which they expressed opinions on the current frequencies, was the closest thing to review. The typical non-committal opinion reflected status quo.

A solid background in data processing applications had put Ray in quick contact with the company controller. He was the first man to turn to for help. Together, they set up a cost trend report based on available cost information from the past five years. (Monthly cost reports had been in use for some time, but there was no further history maintained.) The same procedure was followed for downtime, with a report resulting which listed total downtime for the past two years. (Downtime was kept only for that period of time.)

From these two reports, a list was drawn of all equipment with annual costs over $1,000 and/or downtime over fifty hours. A rough schedule was derived, as follows, and the code noted for each machine.

1. $10,000 and/or 200 hours downtime: monthly.
2. $10,000–$5,000 and/or 200–150 hours: every two months.

3. $5,000–$3,000 and/or 150–100 hours: every quarter.
4. $3,000–$2,000 and/or 100–75 hours: every six months.
5. $2,000–$1,000 and/or 75–50 hours: annually.

The next step involved review of randomly selected monthly cost reports for each piece of equipment. The purpose of this review was to determine if there was an unusual pattern to cost and/or downtime accumulation. For example, if a machine incurred a large expense for a routine annual overhaul, this large annual expense would not necessarily indicate monthly preventive maintenance inspections. On the other hand, a machine that, month in month out, generates considerable downtime with a resulting annual total of 250 hours, is a candidate for a monthly preventive maintenance inspection.

After the rough list had been modified, copies were distributed to each maintenance foreman, with instructions to review each machine carefully, with an eye toward any unusual inspection requirements which would alter the frequency shown on the rough list. Check lists were to be reviewed to assist in identifying these exceptions. For example, a machine might require a vital part to be removed and cleaned each month, although maintenance cost and downtime would indicate only a six months' preventive maintenance check. These requirements were added as separate entries to the rough list.

So as to leave no stone unturned, Ray reviewed the entire equipment identification list with the maintenance and production superintendents. They coded each unit according to the following:

1. *Extremely critical* to operation: breakdown would cause major shut-down of large segment of plant
2. *Critical* to operation: breakdown would cause shut-down of a major part of a department.
3. *Important* to operation: breakdown would cause shut-down of a segment of a department
4. *Interchangeable* in operation: breakdown would cause minor inconvenience in change to alternate equipment

These criticality identifications were then added to the rough list and the current inspection frequency correlated to make sure operational needs were being protected. A "time to schedule" was needed to assist the computer in writing the schedule:

1. Schedule any time
2. Schedule second or third shift
3. Schedule third shift only
4. Schedule weekends only

The rough list with preventive maintenance frequency, maintenance cost/downtime code, and criticality code was then given to the data processing section for compilation of a schedule. Written into the program was the restriction on scheduling any machines with the same two initial digits in the same day. This prevented shutting down too much of a department at one time.

The last item remaining was the standard time required for each inspection. The computer, using past labor input cards, easily calculated an average time for each inspection. Ray, arbitrarily, wrote in an increase of 25% for each to reflect the tighter control of the inspection procedures he contemplated.

Each piece of equipment selected for preventive maintenance now had a card punched with the information necessary to form the schedule. A program was written to schedule, by week, the preventive maintenance required for the equipment. The schedule considered:

1. inspection interval
2. workload balance by maintenance man-hours (The inspections were distributed as evenly as possible within the confines of the frequencies.)
3. departmental downtime (This was distributed evenly so no one section would be burdened unevenly by downtime.)
4. exception times (Some equipment could only be down at certain times.)

Check lists. With a strong, realistic schedule to work from, Ray now turned to the inspections themselves. The first step (and the longest and most tedious of the entire preventive maintenance program) was a review of check lists. This, he felt, was the real heart of the problem of ineffective inspections. Check lists in current use were much too general and, at best, served as a ticket of admission and general guide to the machine. For example, a lathe check list would include inspect headstock; inspect carriage; check motors; etc.

Key maintenance men and supervisors were brought into the picture at this time to provide specific inspection items. "With contribution comes cooperation" was a strong secondary motive for involving as many maintenance men as possible.

Ray tried, wherever possible, to maintain a standardized list for similar machines. Rather than note a few individual differences as exceptions on a standard check list, he soon found it was easier to develop individual lists for equipment that were similar to others but which had a few important exceptional items for inspection.

Wording was definitely standardized throughout: *Inspect* meant inspect visually; *Check* meant some operation of the inspected part was required. Wording was brief because Ray contemplated computer-produced inspection work order cards with pre-printed inspection steps. For this reason, also, mechanical-, electrical-, plumbing-type, etc., work was separated on the check list. The eventual computer system would produce a separate pre-printed work order for each trade group.

Examples of new entries on the check list are: operate headstock and check for unusual noise and vibration; inspect headstock gears and bearings for excessive wear and play; operate carriage in all operations and check for excessive lever and bushing play; blow out to clean, inspect bearings, brushes, and commercial engines (larger, open, and DC motors listed); operate and check for excessive noise and vibration (smaller, enclosed induction motors listed).

Inspection Methods. With a realistic schedule and thorough check lists, Ray was confident the men's inspections would improve. But, to be sure, he instituted a procedure requiring foremen to spot check completed check lists with the men; go over items they had written up; and write work order requests for work required. Where manpower allowed and where workload demanded, he selected men, full time, for inspection work. He soon found that some men adapt very well to inspections, while others would as soon not have anything to do with them. Even the full-time inspectors were rotated to make sure no one was on the same job too long. The inspectors soon developed pride in the performance of their assigned machines and let it be known loud and clear when a write-up was not cleared well enough or soon enough.

Follow-up. In addition to internal action by the inspectors to insure action, a higher priority was given to inspection work orders. While the nature of the work might not justify the high priority, the successful revitalization of the preventive maintenance program did. Ray had to show results to his management, his supervisors, and to his maintenance men.

A backlog report was set up with data processing, noting each preventive maintenance inspection and each resulting work order. These cards were kept separately. Each pre-printed preventive maintenance work order card or following work order card was sent to EDP and the completed cards were sorted weekly against the backlog cards. The remainder were printed on a preventive maintenance backlog report. This report showed equipment number, work order number, and a brief description of work.

By the time Val Salerno retired, Ray had the beginnings of a strong preventive maintenance program and, therefore, the backbone of a strong maintenance department. To maintain this strength, he knew he must continually police the program and periodically provide a thorough review of equipment selection, schedule, and check lists.

VI. Equipment History

Analysis of Codes

Very well summarized by one maintenance manager is the important role of computerized equipment history records:

> Records must be such that Trouble (high cost) areas can be highlighted in a timely manner. We are able to get a print-out of exactly what was done, and can properly interpret efforts expended on specific equipment because we have standardized words and phrases. Merely writing down the correct digits on a card enables the machine to print-out the exact description of work. This is much cheaper than clerical transcribing, interpretation, and typing. It is this that has been, perhaps, the greatest benefit of our D. P. system.[1]

The basis of a machine-operated system history is standardized phrases for trouble-reported and -corrective action. The United States Air Force has used this system for several years. While the process involves some detail, the major trouble and correction can be well identified with a thorough code listing. Any detail necessary for immediate communication to the foreman and manager can be written on the back of the work order card.

We mentioned previously that on the basic work card there is a block for a trouble code and a block for an action code. The trouble code summarizes the work required for the purpose of system histories. Examples of such trouble codes are "P.M.," "stopped," "mis-

---

1. R. R. Costales, "Adapting Data Processing to Preventive Maintenance," *Techniques of Plant Engineering and Maintenance,* Vol. XV (New York: Clapp and Poliak, 1964), p. 78.

aligned," "broken," "out of adjustment," "shorted," "overfilled," and numerous others which apply to a particular operation.

The action code is the more significant, from the standpoint of historical analysis. There are a number of ways to code "action taken," but, basically, any one must satisfy two requirements: describe what was done, and to which equipment it was done. For example, the trouble code on a work order for a large complex machine might stand for leaking. This doesn't mean much by itself, nor does the action code, tighten. But, when we add a component or item code that represents "boring coolant pump," we can pretty well put the whole picture together.

Another code which should be included on the labor reporting or work order card is a service code. This provides a useful report and analysis of the type of work the department is called upon to perform. Examples of such codes are: "P.M.," "routine repair," "break-down," "construction," "modification," "installation," "routine service," etc. Figure 6-1 shows some examples of action and item codes.[2]

From a personnel standpoint, the code system requires considerable management effort to insure that the codes are used correctly. The codes should be posted at time clocks, or, if job times are filled in manually and/or at remote locations, the codes should be printed and placed in plasticized cards so that the men can carry them in their pockets.

As in a manual system, where we have the problem of a man writing too little meaningful information, in a coded system we must insure that the men take enough time to select the *most* meaningful code. General codes, such as "repair," should be avoided because they will be overworked to the exclusion of more specific codes.

How is this reluctance to document the cards properly counteracted? A sample report should be printed, and its use and application thoroughly explained to every maintenance man. This is done, preferably, in small groups, where the maintenance manager can best draw out questions and judge reactions to the program. Each man must be sold on the idea that the report is to help him in his job and that the

2. *Ibid.*

Fig. 6–1: Examples of Action and Item Codes

AIR CONDITIONING REPAIR CODES

CARD CODE 01

Column 1 – Action

	15 - Charged	39 - Purged
	17 - Cleaned	40 - Rebuilt
	18 - Cleared	41 - Regulated
	19 - Closed	42 - Relieved
	20 - Corrected	43 - Relocated
	21 - Defrosted	44 - Removed
	22 - Disassembled	45 - Repaired
	23 - Dried Out	46 - Repiped
	25 - Evacuated	47 - Replaced
	26 - Exchanged	49 - Reseated
	27 - Fabbod New	50 - Reset
	28 - Freed Up	51 - Reversed
02 - Added Refrig.	29 - Insulate	53 - Secured
03 - Added Oil	30 - Lapped Seal	54 - See
05 - Adjusted	31 - Lubricated	55 - Soldered
06 - Aligned	32 - Modified	56 - Started
07 - Assisted	33 - Opened	57 - Stopped
09 - Balanced	34 - Operated	58 - Tested
11 - Calibrated	35 - Ordered Parts	59 - Tightened
13 - Call Foreman	37 - Overhaul	60 - Welded
14 - Changed	38 - Passed On	

Column 2 – Item

01 - Baffle	16 - Coupling	31 - Fly Wheel
02 - Base	17 - Damper	32 - Freon
03 - Bearing	18 - Diffuser	33 - Guard
04 - Belt	19 - Discharge Valve	34 - Header
05 - By Pass	20 - Drain	35 - Heat. Coil
06 - Cascade	21 - Drier	36 - Htr. Element
07 - Chamber	22 - Evap. Cond.	37 - Housing
08 - Chiller	23 - Evap. Cooler	38 - Ice Maker
09 - Coil	24 - Exp. Joint	39 - Insulation
10 - Compressor	25 - Exp. Valve	40 - Inter. Cooler
11 - Conn. Rod	26 - Extractor	41 - Material
12 - Con. Press Reg.	27 - Fan	42 - Modu. Valve
13 - Control	28 - Felt Strip	43 - Motor
14 - Cooling Coil	29 - Filter	44 - Piston
15 - Cooling Tower	30 - Flex Conn.	45 - Planum

AIR CONDITIONING REPAIR CODES (Continued)

CARD CODE 01

Column 2 - Item (Continued)

46 - Prevent. Maint.	58 - Rotor	70 - Thermocouple
47 - Pump	59 - Sched. Maint.	71 - Thermostat
48 - Ram Air Unit	60 - Seal	72 - Unloader
49 - Receiver	61 - Sen. Element	73 - Valve
50 - Refrigerant	62 - Shaft	74 - Valve (Plate)
51 - Refrigerator	63 - Sight Glass	75 - Valve (Serv.)
52 - Refrig. Piping	64 - Solenoid	76 - Vent
53 - Refrig. Unit	65 - Steam Con.	77 - Vibr. Elim.
54 - Regulator	66 - Strainer	78 - Water Cooler
55 - Relief Valve	67 - Suction Valve	79 - Water Pan
56 - Rings	68 - Surge Tank	
57 - Rod	69 - Tank	

PLUMBING REPAIR CODES

CARD CODE 02

Column 1 - Action

	13 - Cleared	34 - Rebuilt
	14 - Closed	35 - Regulated
	15 - Disassembled	37 - Relocated
	17 - Dried Out	38 - Removed
	18 - Evacuated	39 - Repacked
	19 - Exchanged	40 - Repaired
	20 - Fabricated New	41 - Repiped
	21 - Freed Up	42 - Replaced
	22 - Ground Seal	43 - Reseated
	23 - Inspected	44 - Reset
	25 - Insulated	45 - Secured
	26 - Lighted	46 - See
02 - Adjusted	27 - Lubricated	47 - Soldered
03 - Assisted	28 - Opened	49 - Started
05 - Call Foreman	29 - Ordered Parts	50 - Stopped
06 - Capped	30 - Overhaul	51 - Tested
07 - Caulked	31 - Plugged	53 - Tightened
09 - Charged	32 - Primed	54 - Vented
11 - Cleaned	33 - Purged	55 - Welded

PLUMBING REPAIR CODES (Continued)

CARD CODE 02

Column 2 – Item

01 - Acid System	20 - Fuel System	39 - Shaft
02 - Bearings	21 - Gas Burner	40 - Sight Glass
03 - Boiler	22 - Gas Heater	41 - Siphon
04 - Bubbler Valve	23 - Heater Coil	42 - Solenoid Valve
05 - Burner	24 - Hose	43 - Space Heater
06 - By Pass	25 - Housing	44 - Spray Head
07 - Check Valve	26 - Hub	45 - Steam Con.
08 - Chemical Sys.	27 - Material	46 - Steam Heater
09 - Coil	28 - Motor Valve	47 - Stop Valve
10 - Cooling Tower	29 - Micro Mot. Feed	48 - Strainer
11 - Couplings	30 - Nozzle	49 - Supply Pan
12 - Drain	31 - Piping	50 - Tank
13 - Drier	32 - Prevent. Maint.	51 - Test Chamber
14 - Empeller	33 - Pump	52 - Thermocouple
15 - Evap. Cond.	34 - Reg. Valve	53 - Water Cooler
16 - Exp. Joint	35 - Relief Valve	54 - Water Heater
17 - Filter	36 - Sched. Maint.	55 - Water Softener
18 - Float Valve	37 - Seal	
19 - Flash Tank	38 - Seat	

MECHANICAL REPAIR CODES

CARD CODE 03

Column 1 – Action

	09 - Burned	26 - Leveled
	11 - Changed	27 - Machined
	13 - Checked	28 - Metal Sprayed
	14 - Cleaned	29 - Modified
	15 - Closed	30 - Opened
	17 - Corrected	31 - Ordered
	18 - Covered	32 - Performed
	19 - Disassembled	33 - Pump Out
	20 - Emptied	34 - Rebuilt
03 - Adjusted	21 - Fabricated	35 - Refilled
05 - Assembled	22 - Ground	37 - Repacked
06 - Assisted	23 - Inspected	38 - Repaired
07 - Balanced	25 - Installed	39 - Replaced

MECHANICAL REPAIR CODES (Continued)

CARD CODE 03

Column 1 – Action (Continued)

40 - Scraped	43 - Sheet Metal Work	46 - Tested
41 - Serviced	44 - Soldered	47 - Welded
42 - Sharpened	45 - Steam Clean	

Column 2 – Item

01 - A/C Craft	34 - Filter	67 - Pulley
02 - Air System	35 - Fire House Eq.	68 - Pulping Mach.
03 - Alignment	36 - Frame	69 - Pump
04 - Apron Assy.	37 - Furnace	70 - Rollaway
05 - Bearings	38 - Garage Craft	71 - Rolling Stock
06 - Belts	39 - Gas System	72 - Roof
07 - Blue Printer	40 - Gate	73 - Saddle
08 - Boiler	41 - Gear Train	74 - Sander
09 - Brake	42 - Generator	75 - Saw
10 - Building	43 - Grinder	76 - Sched. Maint.
11 - Cabinet	44 - Guard	77 - Seal
12 - Cafe Carte	45 - Gutter	78 - Sewer System
13 - Chamber	46 - Hardware	79 - Shaft
14 - Clutch	47 - Head Stock	80 - Shear
15 - Compressor	48 - Hoist	81 - Signs
16 - Coolant Sys.	49 - Hood	82 - Small Tools
17 - Cooling Tower	50 - Hydra. Sys.	83 - Spindle Assy.
18 - Coupling	51 - Instruments	84 - Spray Booth
19 - Cross Slide	52 - Knee Assy.	85 - Steam System
20 - Cylinder	53 - Lab. Equip.	86 - Sub-Station
21 - Degreaser	54 - Lathe	87 - Supply System
22 - Door	55 - Locking Bar	88 - Table
23 - Drill	56 - Lube System	89 - Tailstock
24 - Drive Assy.	57 - Mill	90 - Tank
25 - Duct	58 - Motor	91 - Trash Carts
26 - Elect. Craft	59 - Nut & Screw	92 - Tubing
27 - Elect. Sys.	60 - Office Equip.	93 - Vacuum Sys.
28 - Elevator	61 - Oven	94 - Water System
29 - Engine	62 - Parking Lot	95 - Welder
30 - Equipment	63 - Parts	96 - Whys
21 - Exhaust Sys.	64 - Plumbing Craft	97 - Window
32 - Fan	65 - Press	
33 - Fence	66 - Prevent. Maint.	

ELECTRICAL REPAIR CODES

CARD CODE 04

Column 1 – Action

02 - Adjusted
03 - Aligned
05 - Assembled
06 - Balanced
07 - Calibrated

09 - Cleaned
11 - Corrected
13 - Disassembled
14 - Hypotted
15 - Inspected
17 - Installed
18 - Insulated
19 - Inverted
20 - Lube'd
21 - Maintenance
22 - Meggared
23 - Moved
25 - Ordered
26 - Overhaul (Maj.)
27 - Overhaul (Min.)
28 - Pumped
29 - Record

30 - Reinstall
31 - Relamped
32 - Repaired
33 - Replaced
34 - Reset
35 - Reversed
37 - Rewound
38 - Scaled
39 - See
40 - Soldered
41 - Spliced
42 - Straighten
43 - Surveyed
44 - Tested
45 - Tightened

Column 2 – Item

01 - Alternator
02 - Amplifier
03 - Battery
04 - Bearings
05 - Booth
06 - Brake
07 - Breaker
08 - Brushes
09 - Capacitor
10 - Chamber
11 - Charger
12 - Circuit
13 - Clearance
14 - Clutch
15 - Coil
16 - Collector
17 - Commutator
18 - Compressor

19 - Computer
20 - Condensor
21 - Conduit
22 - Contacts
23 - Control
24 - Cover
25 - Current
26 - Dishwasher
27 - Disposal
28 - Distr., Prim.
29 - Dist., 400 Cy.
30 - Dist., 1600 Cy.
31 - Dist., 28 V.DC
32 - Elect. Sys.
33 - Electro-Plating
34 - Element
35 - Elevator
36 - Exciter

37 - Fan
38 - Feeder
39 - Frequency
40 - Furnace
41 - Generator
42 - Cutter
43 - Heater
44 - Hoist
45 - Insulation
46 - Instrument
47 - Leads
48 - Machine
49 - Mach. Light
50 - Magnet
51 - Material
52 - Motor
53   MG Set
54 - Motor

ELECTRICAL REPAIR CODES (Continued)

CARD CODE 04

Column 2 – Item (Continued)

55 - OCD	68 - Regulator	81 - Switchgear
56 - OFC	69 - Relay-Mag. Switch	82 - Temperature
57 - Oven	70 - Resistor	83 - Thermocouple
58 - Panel	71 - Rheostat	84 - Thermostat
59 - Parts	72 - Rotor	85 - Time Clock
60 - Pressure	73 - Secondary	86 - Time Stamp
61 - Prev. Maint.	74 - Sched. Maint.	87 - Timer
62 - Projector	75 - Small Tool Repair	88 - Transformer
63 - Pump	76 - Solenoids	89 - Tube
64 - Push Button	77 - Speaker	90 - Valve
65 - Recorder	78 - Starter	91 - Voltage
66 - Rectifier	79 - Sub Station	92 - Welder
67 - Refrigerator	80 - Switch	93 - Winding

GARAGE REPAIR CODES

CARD CODE 05

Column 1 – Action

	05 - Appraised	23 - Perform
	06 - Assembled	25 - Pick-Up
	07 - Balance	26 - Polish
	09 - Cleaned	27 - Remove
	11 - Deliver	28 - Repair
	13 - Disassembled	29 - Replace
	14 - Gassing	30 - Rotate
	15 - Inspect	31 - See
	17 - Install	32 - Service
	18 - Lubricate	33 - Steam Clean
	19 - Maintenance	34 - Towed
	20 - Operate	35 - Tune-Up
02 - Adjust	21 - Overhaul (Maj.)	37 - Wash (Off Premise)
03 - Align	22 - Overhaul (Min.)	38 - Wash (On Premise)

GARAGE REPAIR CODES (Continued)

CARD CODE 05

Column 2 – Item

01 - 1,000 Mile	24 - Fire Truck	47 - Sedan
02 - 2,000 Mile	25 - Fleet	48 - Service Truck
03 - 5,000 Mile	26 - Flood Control	49 - Shop Maint.
04 - 40/50 Hours	27 - Forklift	50 - Speedometer-Clocks
05 - Ambulance	28 - Garage Equip.	51 - Starter
06 - Battery	29 - Gas Pump	52 - Stat. Equipment
07 - Bicycle	30 - Gas Truck	53 - Station Wagon
08 - Body & Fender	31 - Generator	54 - Steering
09 - Brakes	32 - Glass	55 - Tarpaulin
10 - Bus	33 - Heater	56 - Tires
11 - Cafe. Carts	34 - Ignition	57 - Toby Cart
12 - Carburetor	35 - Jeep	58 - Tow Truck
13 - Carry All	36 - Kalamazoo	59 - Transmission
14 - Chassis	37 - Material	60 - Trash Cart
15 - Clutch	38 - Misc. Parts	61 - Truck
16 - Cooling Sys.	39 - Off Prem. (Fleet)	62 - Tug
17 - Defroster	40 - Personnel	63 - Universal Joints
18 - Differential	41 - Portable Equip.	64 - Vehicle
19 - Elect. System	42 - Prev. Maint.	65 - Water Truck
20 - Emerg. Equip.	43 - Radio	66 - Wheels
21 - Emerg. Truck	44 - 2 Way Radio	67 - Wheel Bearing
22 - Engine	45 - Rolling Stock	68 - Wind. Washer
23 - Exhaust Sys.	46 - Sched. Maint.	69 - Wind. Wipers

KEY FOR IDENTIFYING MACHINE TOOL REPAIRS

Part 1 *Electrical–Sub-Assemblies*	*Part 1-A* *Electrical–Parts*	*Part 3* *Reason for Repair*
01 - Apron	01 - Arc shield	01 - Dirt–Oil–Moisture
02 - Battery	02 - Armature	02 - Fatigue
03 - Brake	03 - Belts	03 - Incorrect set-up
04 - Brazer	04 - Blades	04 - Incorr. lubrication
05 - Breaker	05 - Brushes	05 - Improper setting
06 - Clutch	06 - Brush holder	06 - Improper use
07 - Controller	07 - Ballast	07 - Installation
08 - Distributor	08 - Battery solution	08 - Lack of lubrication
09 - Electrical Alarm	09 - Carbon	09 - Misalignment
10 - Furnace-oven	10 - Cell	10 - Modify

KEY FOR IDENTIFYING MACHINE TOOL REPAIRS (Continued)

Part 1 *Electrical–Sub-Assemblies*	*Part 1-A* *Electrical–Parts*	*Part 3* *Reason for Repair*
11 - Generator	11 - Clock motor	11 - Normal wear
12 - Light fixture	12 - Collector	12 - Overheating
13 - Magnets	13 - Commutator	13 - Overload
14 - Meter	14 - Compartment	14 - Out of balance
15 - Motor	15 - Conduit	15 - Shorted
16 - Push button	16 - Connectors	16 - Wrong material
17 - Rectox	17 - Contacts	
18 - Recorder & Controls	18 - Coils	
19 - Relay	19 - Electrode	
20 - Rheostat	20 - Fan	
21 - Rolls	21 - Finger	
22 - Starter	22 - Fittings	
23 - Switch	23 - Fuse	
24 - Switch-limit	24 - Handle	
25 - Transformer	25 - Heater element	
26 - Timer	26 - Insulation	
27 - Tap changer	27 - Insulator	
28 - Valve	28 - Lamp	
29 - Welder	29 - Leads	
30 - Other	30 - Oil	
	31 - Plates	
	32 - Plunger	
	33 - Plug	
	34 - Resistor	
	35 - Rotor	
	36 - Screw	
	37 - Shunt	
	38 - Solenoid	
	39 - Socket	
	40 - Spring	
	41 - Terminals	
	42 - Thermocouple	
	43 - Thermostat	
	44 - Tongs	
	45 - Tube	
	46 - Wire or cable	
	47 - Complete unit	
	48 - Others	

KEY FOR IDENTIFYING MACHINE TOOL REPAIRS (Continued)

Part 2 *Mechanical—* *Sub-Assemblies*	*Part 2A* *Mechanical—* *Parts*	*Part 3* *Reason for Repair*
	01 - Adjusting screw	01 - Dirt—Oil—Moisture
	02 - Arm	02 - Fatigue
	03 - Band	03 - Incorrect set-up
	04 - Beam	04 - Incorrect lubrication
	05 - Bearing	05 - Improper setting
	06 - Belt	06 - Improper use
	07 - Blades	07 - Installation
	08 - Bracket	08 - Lack of lubrication
	09 - Bucket	09 - Misalignment
	10 - Bumper	10 - Modify
	11 - Bushing	11 - Normal wear
	12 - Cable	12 - Overheating
	13 - Cam	13 - Overload
	14 - Cam shaft	14 - Out of balance
	15 - Chain	15 - Shorted
	16 - Chutes	16 - Wrong material
	17 - Clamp	
	18 - Clapper	
	19 - Coil	
	20 - Connecting rod	
	21 - Coupling	
	22 - Cups	
	23 - Crank shaft	
	24 - Diaphragm	
	25 - Disc	
	26 - Dog	
	27 - Drive shaft	
	28 - Filter	
	29 - Finger	
	30 - Fluid	
	31 - Forks	
	32 - Gasket	
	33 - Gear	
	34 - Gib	
	35 - Guide	
	36 - Guard	
	37 - Gauge	
	38 - Handle	
	39 - Hook	
	40 - Hoppers	
41 - Apron	41 - Hose	
42 - Arm Assembly	42 - Horn	
43 - Air control	43 - Impeller	

KEY

KEY FOR IDENTIFYING MACHINE TOOL REPAIRS (Continued)

Part 2 *Mechanical —* *Sub-Assemblies*	*Part 2A* *Mechanical —* *Parts*	*Part 3* *Reason for Repair*
44 - Base	44 - Lever	
45 - Bridge	45 - Line shaft	
46 - Brake	46 - Lining	
47 - Bed	47 - Link	
48 - Boom	48 - Mast	
49 - Carriage	49 - Nut	
50 - Clutch	50 - Nozzle	
51 - Column	51 - Packing	
52 - Coolant system	52 - Pedal	
53 - Cross rail	53 - Pins	
54 - Cross slide	54 - Pintle	
55 - Crank shaft	55 - Piping	
56 - Cylinder	56 - Piston	
57 - Drive	57 - Plate	
58 - Drum	58 - Platforms	
59 - Electrode	59 - Plug	
60 - Fan	60 - Pulley	
61 - Face plate	61 - Rack	
62 - Feed box	62 - Ram	
63 - Feed mechanism	63 - Retainer	
64 - Frame	64 - Rings	
65 - Head	65 - Rolls	
66 - Housing	66 - Shaft	
67 - Hoist	67 - Sheaves	
68 - Knee	68 - Shifter	
69 - Motor	69 - Slide	
70 - Pump	70 - Sleeve	
71 - Ram	71 - Spring	
72 - Regulator	72 - Screw—lead—feed	
73 - Saddle	73 - Strainer	
74 - Spindle	74 - Tires	
75 - Steering mechanism	75 - Toggle	
76 - Stock feed	76 - Tubing	
77 - Support (out post)	77 - Valve	
78 - Table	78 - Ways	
79 - Tanks	79 - Wheel	
80 - Tail Stock	80 - Worm	
81 - Trolley	81 - Complete Unit	
82 - Truck	82 - Others	
83 - Turret		
84 - Unreelers		
85 - Others		

reports are available to *him* at any time for use in analyzing a piece of equipment's past problems.

For the still uninspired (more than likely the majority), it will just take a lot of checking and correction by the foreman until the procedure becomes natural practice to the men involved. An important point here is consistency. As a questionable coding situation arises, it should be studied carefully by the maintenance manager and a decision should be made which he may want reflected in future reports. Any confusion on management's part will alienate the men from system quicker than if it were being paid for out of their pockets.

While this seems to be a lot of detail and seemingly common sense management practice, we cannot overemphasize the importance of correct input data to any EDP system. *Systems have failed or are working at less than optimum effectiveness just because management has not taken the trouble to bring into the picture, initially and continuously, the man who generates the data.*

Reports Using Codes

There are several ways to include repair codes in the form of reports. The basic purpose is for the equipment history record. This replaces the manually posted equipment records and takes the following form:

Activity Identification (Machine)	*Month-Year*	*Type of Service*	*Trouble Code*	*Item Code*	*Action Code*
		(*this is optional*)			

This annual report serves as the historical report for that piece of equipment. In addition, the trouble, item, and action codes can be added to the monthly labor cost report on which each work order and cost is listed. This report is the one used for interim problem and trend analysis.

There are other special reports which can be generated from the coding data. Examples of such reports are: a report listing all instances of a particular item, such as "selector switch," failing on all machines; or, a report of all uses of one particular action code, such as "replace brushes" or "replace belts."

While the code we have does not always *exactly* describe the situation, on the other hand, the codes enable us to achieve standardization of data. Anyone who has pored over manually posted history cards looking for a particular problem, and found it written in a dozen different ways, will appreciate a report in which he can scan a column of numbers and pick out the occurrences in question.

CASE STUDY V: "THREE YEARS AGO, THE SAME THING."

Bud Barret fought a continual battle against a very unstable temper. He was a greatly skilled maintenance superintendent, who inspired his men by moving in the right direction. The day the muller broke down for the third week in succession was not one of his even-tempered days.

He had the mechanical and electrical foremen on the carpet within minutes: "You guys get that (—) muller fixed and keep it fixed or move out of the foremen's locker-room!"

Jim Petrocelli, the mechanical foreman, had about had it with the muller problem and now with his boss: "We're doing the best we can. Now you fix the (—) muller yourself. I'm moving."

Repeat problems are *the* most unsettling situation for a maintenance department. A first-time problem presents the "under-the-gun" challenge that attracts and holds all maintenance people. But, repeat write-ups are direct slaps at the department, its supervisors, and the men working last on the job. Management pressures intensify exponentially at repeat write-ups, and this impetus is carried down to the men. Production workers, also, have been known to be unmerciful under these circumstances.

Because the cause of some problems, particularly those involving electrical or electronic controls, is not readily apparent, the maintenance department leaves itself wide open to repeats with trial and error methods. How best to identify the pattern and circumstances under which a malfunction occurs? A history of past, similar conditions is the most direct way.

The absence of a good history system soon became apparent to Ed McPhillister, the production manager, when Bud Barret had calmed down enough to take his problem to his boss. Ed reasoned that part of the short tempers in the maintenance department stemmed from a feeling of helplessness and a lack of confidence in the management tools provided. A

Fig. 6–2: Information Flow: Equipment History

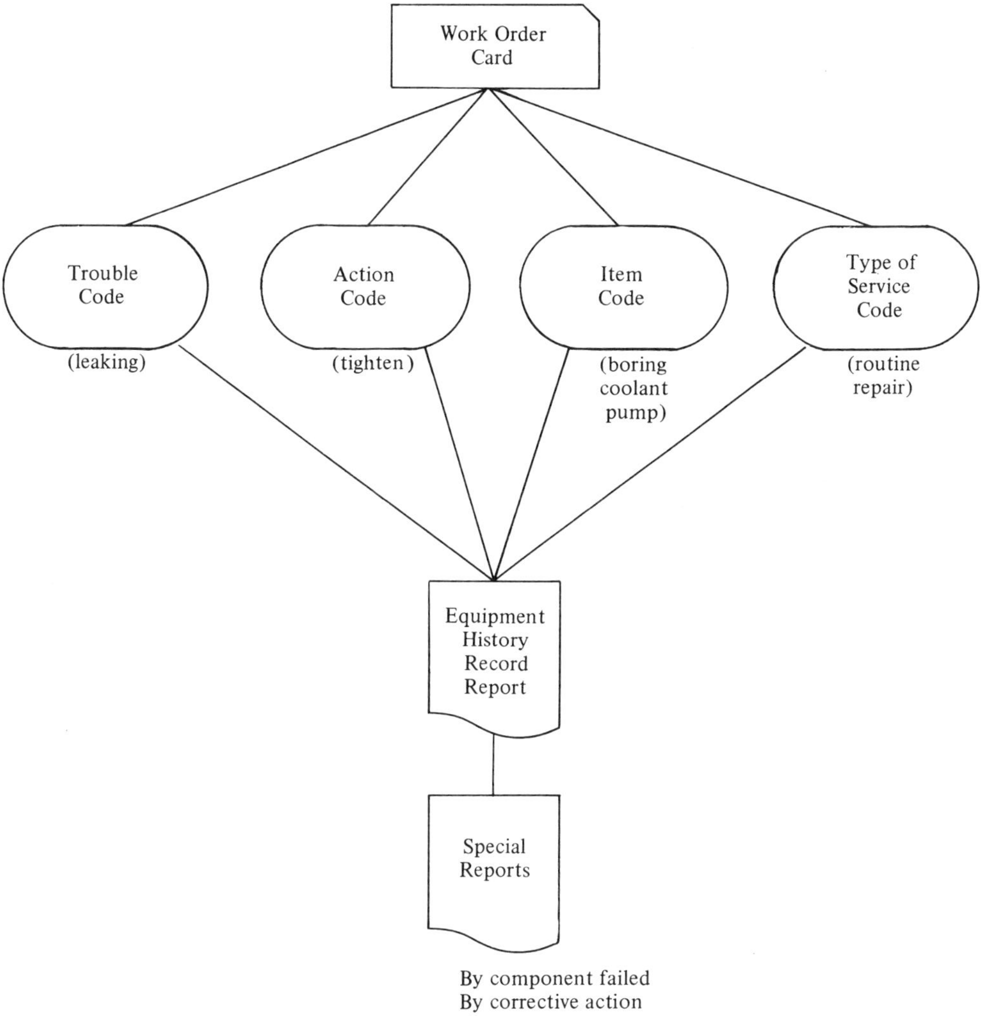

system was a bother to keep up when everything was running smoothly, but a very necessary thing when the chips were down (or the muller, for the third time!).

Ed knew he had a two-fold problem: (1) to develop a system of past history for most machines, which, even if not providing an immediate solution, would, at least, get his supervisors to sit down and think analytically about their problems; and, (2) to convince the men to use the system.

The company had adequate data processing facilities, a work order system with cost reporting, and a downtime system. The nearest thing to an equipment history was a file of work orders set up by machine number.

Figuring this was the best place to start, Ed had the muller file brought to his office, and called his superintendent and the two foremen. Together, they went through the file, and it was Bob Conkle, the electrical foreman, who came across a work order with almost the same circumstances over three years ago. The corrective action at that time (by a second shift electrician, since departed) was to replace an erratic component in the additive control unit. A call to the shop had the muller making good sand again within a half hour.

Ed had made his point. The next hour was spent outlining requirements for a more usable equipment history system. Prime requirements were that the system be: (1) easy to use; (2) easy to maintain; and (3) meaningful to the maintenance man.

The next day, Bud Barret met with the company controller, Dan Boger, and a history report was developed, based on malfunction and corrective action codes. Bud's assignment was to come up with the list of codes and the general format of the report he wanted. There was adequate space on the present work order for inclusion of the codes. Eventually, the controller would recommend a pre-punched work order card to eliminate the additional key punching for the report.

A call to the data processing equipment representative brought standard lists of codes. From these, Bud and his staff added and subtracted until they had compiled codes for every imaginable *trouble reported* and *corrective action*. They were later to find that conditions would arise that would require further additions, but they had a good start.

Key groups of maintenance people were brought in on meetings to establish codes, so the system was no surprise to the maintenance crew when it was introduced. For a while, they were asked to continue writing out the corrective action as before and to note the corrective action code. Code application was checked very carefully by front line supervisors and spot-checked by Bud and Ed. Corrections were made immediately and brief memos were posted explaining questionable situations. After about three months, the written corrective action was reduced and reliance was mainly on the codes.

The first couple of months saw brief meetings with all the maintenance men, during which the codes were defined in detail. The advantages of the system in repeat conditions and multiple replacements of component parts were pointed out to the men. By scanning for a trouble, action, or item code, the men saw repeat conditions that were not otherwise noted in day-to-day operations. This advantage was particularly important in this fairly large maintenance organization with its multiple shift coverage.

A file was set up in the central maintenance shop where monthly reports were filed. A six-month report was initiated which combined, by machine, all the monthly reports. Maintenance men were encouraged to refer to these reports when stumped by a troublesome malfunction. It would be a few years before the condensed semi-annual and annual reports would be useful to recall someone else's corrective action, but the men who took the time to use the reports soon found that even a few months' past history helped their analyses of the problems.

As Ed suspected, the reluctance of the men to be involved with paper work was no small problem. It became a practice of each front line supervisor to preface any discussion of a problem with a maintenance man by: "Did you check out the record?" A few key discoveries of problem solutions paved the way to more universal acceptance of the equipment histories.

It was enlightening to Bud Barret that the tempers (especially his own) subsided and were better directed, in time of troublesome breakdowns, by analytical study of the history reports. To be able to do something to find a solution that was not obvious was far superior to frustrating trial and error.

VII. Work Standards and Estimates

Work Standards: Advisable?

Maintenance, in general, has been slow to accept standards, for the simple reason that there are a lot of maintenance jobs for which standards cannot be established. There are too many one-of-a-kind tasks filling a good part of every day. Standards are probably more advantageous to a large company or multi-location corporation because it will have more occasion for repetitive work.

Setting standards is a time-consuming and continuous procedure. The computer method can reduce the time and cost involved. EDP will bring costs down to where we can justify the advantages of standards. The normally stated advantages of standards are summed up well in the following quotation:

> Use of data processing equipment for a period of three to six months will show a definite pattern of times for any given operation . . . (which) provides a standard against which work of individual employees can be measured. Any deviation from this historically established standard indicates that corrective action may be necessary. In certain operations of a repetitive nature, a learning curve may be applied to the standard and a continual improvement in efficiency and a lowering of times should be noted.[1]

A related, but different, approach to standards involves the problem of incentive for workers. Without encouraging incentive pay,

1. William J. Smith, "Data Processing by Machine," *Maintenance Engineering Handbook,* 2nd Edition (New York: McGraw-Hill, Inc., 1966). Copyright 1966 by McGraw-Hill, Inc. Used with permission of McGraw-Hill Book Company.

which is totally unacceptable, the very existence of a standard time on a work order card will encourage the man to attain that goal. Experience shows that, in an emergency or really critical situation, an average maintenance man will put out considerably more effort than on normal, scheduled jobs. Why not introduce a method that will place the job outside the category of "routine work which is being done to fill the time between rush jobs"?

We must attempt to make Parkinson's Law of Time Consumption work for us. By applying reasonable standards and by assigning to a man jobs that total a full day's work, we are, in effect, making him a manager. He knows exactly what is expected of him, and it is up to him to manage his work so as to accomplish everything assigned. What he loses on one job, he had better make up on the second. The psychology involved here may seem simple enough, but how many departments, instead, operate from work order to work order? This is where Parkinson's Law can chew up maintenance man-hours at a fierce rate.

We have proposed a system of work assignments which, obviously, depends on a standard time. While we will show how the computer will assist us in establishing standard times, we must realize that we also have to estimate times for a large percentage (50%–75%) of the jobs for which we can't set standards.

Scientific scheduling cannot exist without standards and estimates. General manpower allocation and backlog cannot be assessed accurately without standards and estimates. Is it not logical, then, to conclude that every maintenance work order generated should be assigned a pre-determined standard time or a carefully considered estimated time?

Establishing Standards and Estimates

Available data determine how soon a department can set standards. If an EDP program, with coded work orders, has been in effect for some time, enough data are available. If such a program is just getting started, it will take several months before enough data are generated. Even without coded work orders, however, there may be enough information in old work order files, depending on how much man-hour information is included with them. Considerable effort is required to develop standards by finding comparable work orders and averaging the associated times.

If coded work orders are in existence, it is a simple matter to machine-sort all work orders by designated combinations of codes. For instance, sort out and average all combinations of Action Code-11 (cleaned) and Item Code-22 (gas heater). These combinations will yield an accurate standard for "cleaning gas heaters."

It is also easy to review and update standards on a periodic basis through this procedure. The biggest task initially is determining the code combinations for which we can establish standards. Another look at the types of work discussed previously will show if they are adaptable to standards.

Preventive Maintenance — Routine

Most of these jobs are readily adaptable to standards. Preventive maintenance standards can be made part of the work order printing requirements. The problem encountered is in the multiple work cards needed for each inspection, due to different crafts' working on the same inspection. As mentioned in Chapter V on preventive maintenance, each craft has its own card, or group of cards, and they are coded as follows:

Action Code: Code for preventive maintenance.
Item Code: Code for craft. This craft code tells the computer to reference the craft noted in the designated craft block on the card.

The resulting standards for a particular type of machine will then be shown. Examples:

Electrical Preventive Maintenance: 4.8
Plumbing Preventive Maintenance: 3.2
Mechanical Preventive Maintenance: 6.1

Routine work that is printed from a schedule can also include the standard as part of the work order printing requirements.

Backlog Work

Originating from daily work requests, backlog work is checked for available standards by the scheduler handling the incoming request. If there is a standard, he notes the hours on the request before sending it to EDP for processing of the work order card. If there is no standard, he secures an estimate for the job from the planner or foreman, or whoever is responsible for estimating. Every job in backlog should have a standard or an estimated time.

Some jobs require multiple crafts. This matter is handled in the same manner as the preventive maintenance jobs: a card for each craft with its own estimate of time.

Emergency Work

Unless this type of call-in work fits a standard time or unless it is of a determinable duration and such that it can be estimated, it is not considered as part of the work to be evaluated. A good portion of emergency work involves breakdowns and, where trouble-shooting is involved — electrically or mechanically — time estimates are difficult.

Although they are not classified as bona fide emergencies, we should also consider in this section those "little" jobs performed by every maintenance department — jobs which consume less than an hour's time, but are vital to production (or the boss) and must be done right away. Estimating these jobs would serve no purpose, because their very nature defines the time necessary to accomplish them. Examples of such work are the minor adjustments required by production machinery, or a broken air line.

Note that we are dealing primarily with historical, not engineered, standards. Because maintenance work is so specialized for each given operation and is difficult enough to standardize, it is this writer's belief that published engineered standards are too general for specific use without considerable modification. They are of value only from a reference standpoint insofar as they can be used to identify extremes in an organization's own standards. Here, again, the size of the operation determines the applicability of engineered standards. A large magnitude maintenance group, with enough categorical work, may be able to justify the exploration of engineered standards.

Putting Standards and Estimates to Work

The very implementation of standards is their greatest advantage because it causes foremen and superintendents to look at every job through standard-colored glasses; off-standard jobs soon begin to stand out. A general means to improve work, for which the historical standard appears satisfactory on the surface, is to apply a percentage reduction. Start out with 10%, for example, and, if history proves it possible, reduce the standard time by another 5%. Judgment and consideration of attitudes and morale must be exercised in changing a standard once it is published, whether we are dealing with production work or maintenance jobs.

Once we have established standards and allowed for periodic review, we can begin to apply them. Most standards are predicated on code combinations and can be matched by the computer. There is a basic difference in standard types here which must be mentioned.

We will take the easier type first. There are jobs which are described well enough by the trouble code, or trouble and item combination, to have a standard based on that alone. This standard can be printed on the work order card and is, of course, known to the men.

A second type is an after-the-fact standard which requires an action code. Because the action code is not known until the job is completed, the standard will not be known to the man performing the work. It will appear on the work order report and is just as valuable in performance evaluation.

We can see that job times can be considered and recorded three times. First when the work request is received, it does not fit an obvious, published standard, so the scheduler turns it over to the planner or foreman for estimating. Second, an actual time is added as the job is done; and, third, the action code combination may fit the job to an established standard.

The reader should now visualize three additional columns on the work order report, showing Actual Time, Standard Time, and Estimated Time. These, totalled, will show departmental effectiveness in meeting standards. Separate reports can be drawn from the basic report to show the combinations of actual versus estimated, or actual versus standard, for various activity groups, such as by craft, by plant area, by supervisory group, or even by individual worker (see Figure 7-1). These reports will show not only the ability of men and su-

Fig. 7-1: Format of Standards Report
(Separate or included with Basic Work Order Report)

Identification Number	Work Order Number	Description	Actual Hours	Standard Hours	Estimated Hours
SR 1003	53280	Repr. job cntrl.	8.4	10.0	10.0 (2)
SR 2005	57839	Chng. mtr. brng.	3.2	2.8	2.8
SR 1157	54624	Free limit switch	2.4	–	2.0 (2)
		(Can be grouped by craft, department, etc.)			

pervisors to meet the standard times but, also the effectiveness of estimators in serving their function.

Because many jobs require more than one man, we must provide a prefix to the work order card which indicates when the number required is more than one. The work order report will show the total man-hours estimated or standard versus the total actual man-hours. This tends to support a feeling of teamwork among the men in a craft, especially where different groups are working at different times on the same job with a total time standard.

A modified system for standards evaluation is described in Chapter X, Backlog. This system is used where there is a separate work order rather than the combined card. The report generated is separate, with the same basic information described above or as shown in Figure 7-1.

The reception of a standards system by any group of workers varies as much as people do. However, the consensus will be objection, in varying degrees. In a plant where production workers are on a standard or incentive system, the shock might be mild, depending on the general acceptance of the existing system.

A production standard system, of course, involves minimum outputs and pay rates. While there may be objections to this, it is this writer's feeling that a standards system involving the men's paychecks does not work successfully in a maintenance function.

Maintenance jobs vary so considerably that tying pay to jobs creates more productivity problems than benefits. Maintenance standards should be management tools used by supervisors to measure their own output and that of individual workers. If the program is introduced carefully, and if there is rapport between labor and management, the standards system will assist productivity.

CASE STUDY VI: "COME ON, WE'RE OVER STANDARD NOW."

Joe O'Lorry, with his flair for the flamboyant, must have had some public relations or advertising background. Not only was he a good engineer but he knew his maintenance people and what motivated them. He had worked as a helper in a maintenance group for three summers while going to college.

The corporate industrial engineer decided that Joe's division would attempt negotiated standards in the maintenance department. The ensuing showdown at corporate headquarters between Joe and the industrial engineer was preceded by many days of researching work order reports for identical jobs with varying times. While Joe showed enough variance to convince the corporate staff to retrench their thinking about maintenance pay based on standards, he also convinced himself that there was a sufficient array of tight times to warrant standard assignment as a management tool. He agreed to initiate a system on this basis, partly to judge effectiveness and partly to judge reaction by the maintenance men.

Joe was set up to collate the necessary data with a solid system of work orders, codes, and labor costs. A lot of digging out of old cards by a very cooperative data processing manager, a simple program, and considerable machine sorting provided a starting list of standards. Joe concentrated on preventive maintenance inspections and oft-recurring jobs for a start because the data spread was fairly narrow.

So much for the easy part. Introducing this program to a crew who, to the last man, fancied themselves skilled craftsmen (and a few of them actually were) was an entirely different proposition, although the

Fig. 7–2: Information Flow: Standards

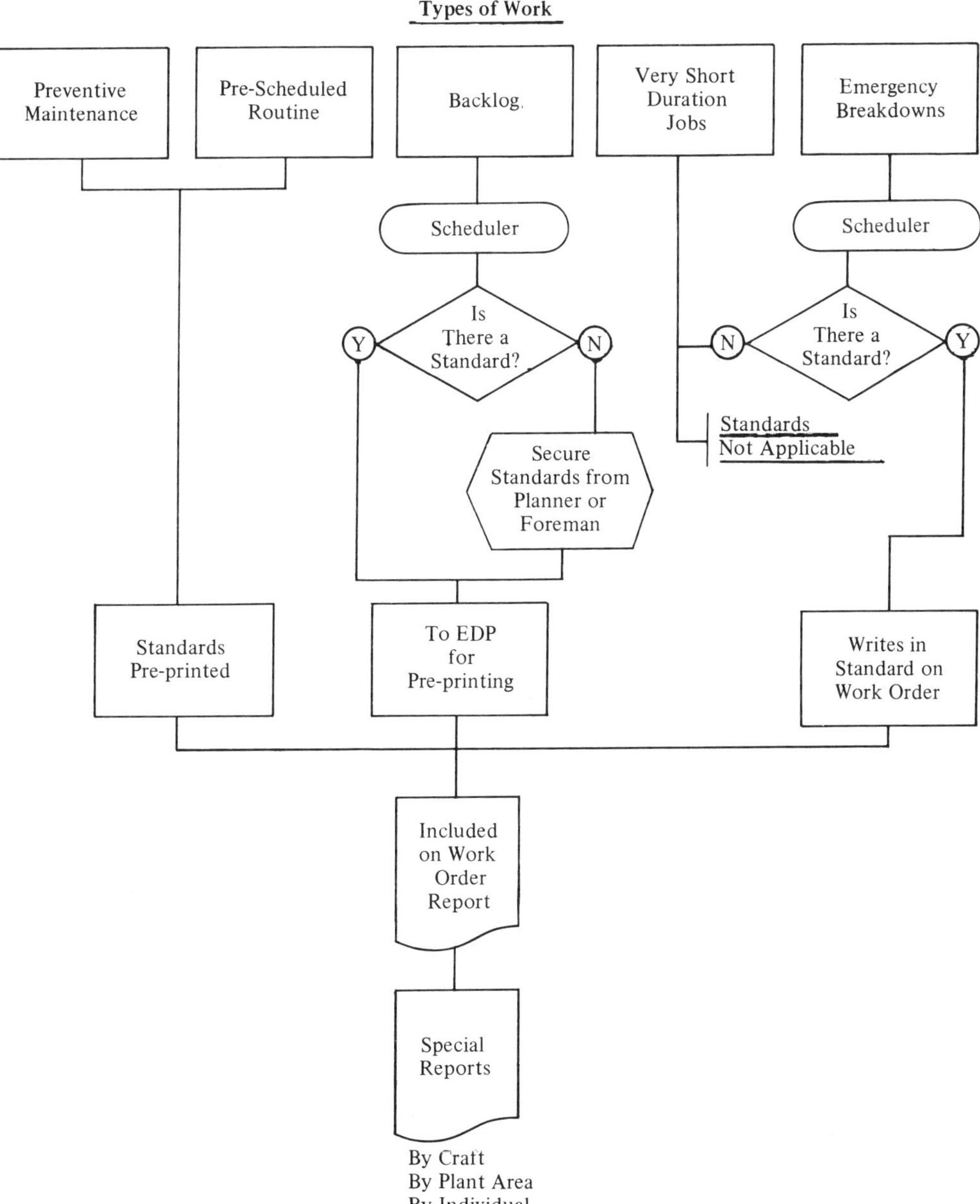

men were used to periodic work samplings and, so, they were not altogether strange to work measurements methods.

The results of his work samplings were in Joe's favor, notwithstanding the fact that he did not have a high rate of productivity. Various changes in work assignments, and shop and stockroom locations had improved his "working" percentage somewhat, but there was still a pretty good-sized lag in productivity. He knew the men knew this, and he counted on this knowledge of potentially greater productivity to cushion the blow of working against the clock.

In a brainstorming session with foremen and superintendents, the alternate motivations were discussed. A few men responded to the mere challenge; the majority needed something more. Another few — the least productive — would forever resent specific measurement of their efforts.

Setting up a competitive system was a good starting point. There was already friendly competition among the craft groups; a scoreboard was set up in the central shop showing standard hours, actual hours, and percent of standard hours for each craft or work group. A company credit for hand tools was to be awarded every two months to each craft group with the best percentage of standard time. There was an annual award of half a day off with pay for the overall winner.

Because a substantial part of the work was on new jobs, the foremen would have to supply pre-job estimates, and, because the foremen were also on a bonus system, there was a possibility of estimating jobs too high to make a better showing. To counter this possibility, a 75% limit as a percentage of standard was established.

Against this background, the system was introduced. It was sold, primarily, as a management tool with which the department could measure its own effectiveness, but it was also a means to identify and reward those men who were producing a good day's work. With some skepticism and with a procedural grievance from the union, the program left the dock.

In an amazingly short time, the whole department became time conscious. The weekly work order reports had to be posted so that the men could follow their progress. The foremen became very much aware of time consumed on routine jobs, and "fill" jobs in between breakdown assignments. In fact, Joe threatened to impose a penalty of "loss time" gained for any repeat write-ups to protect against carelessness by some men, which further helped the program.

By the time the first session winners were announced and the tool certificates distributed, the program was successfully on its way. The union withdrew its objection, and Joe withstood further efforts to impose new pay standards in light of the increased productivity.

VIII. Materials Control

It is in the area of materials control that the most positive control system can be established. Here we are, generally, not concerned with human frailty or unpredictable job times but, rather, with definite numbers and costs of items.

Inventory Control

This field (like others which follow in this chapter) is applicable to corporate functions other than maintenance and, as such, may be instigated by someone other than the maintenance manager. While this is not the place to elaborate on inventory control theory, we must mention that components of the theory, such as re-order points, stock levels, and economic order quantities, are readily adaptable to computer programs for inventory models. While maintenance does not use the dollar's worth of material consumed by the product in a manufacturing concern, we must recognize that there is a great potential for waste in maintenance inventories and, consequently, a great opportunity for cost savings through scientific control.

Perhaps even more important than the conservation of inventory dollars is the protection against parts shortage afforded by computerized inventory control. With a liberal cost for outage applied in the inventory formula, we can be pretty well assured of having that valuable part on hand when we need it.

Operation of Maintenance Materials Control

The basic item in this system is the material requisition card (which is covered in great detail in the previous chapter on installing the basic system). We stress again the need for a card to be completed for every item drawn from inventory.

In addition to the basic information stated by the requisitioner, the stock clerk or someone in accounting will assign a standard cost to the item. This cost is determined by accounting by averaging various invoices for that item. Purchasing can interpret, also, new quotations for the item as additional suppliers are located. These costs and quotations are reviewed periodically and an adjusted standard cost is printed.

Recall that the work order number and activity designation are included on each requisition card. In this way, the current standard cost of all material used will be shown on the work order report for every job.

As the cards come up to the computer function each day, those requisitions are checked against the master inventory list. This "computer inventory file" will not only have the computed economic order point and quantity but, also, the amount of the item on hand. The computer will issue ordering instructions when a stock is due to be replenished. The receiving slip is made up as a data input card and serves to adjust the master inventory list to its proper quantity level (see following, "Memo Describing Maintenance Cost Reporting Procedures"). This system eliminates the need for great stacks of inventory file cards and all associated manual posting.

Anyone associated with maintenance inventory is well aware of the work involved with the initiation and upkeep of a manually posted parts catalog. The computer can readily publish a catalog of every item on its master inventory list. This catalog is normally printed in sequence of the activity identification, which is, most likely, a machine number. Anyone wanting "a front spindle bearing for lathe 1022," goes to the catalog, finds "lathe 1022" in numerical sequence, finds "bearing, front spindle" in alphabetical order under that machine, and notes the bin number in which it can be found.

MEMO DESCRIBING MAINTENANCE COST REPORTING PROCEDURES

To supply the correct information for a new parts and material cost reporting system, we will now follow these procedures:

1. Where applicable, a work order number must appear on each receiving slip. Receiving will obtain the work order number from the purchase order. (Obviously, this work order number must be included on the purchase requisition.) If an item is being ordered for general stock and not for a particular work order, then we will note "no work order" on the requisition and this will be typed on the purchase order.

   The receiving clerk will question the requisitioner about any purchase order which does not have a work order reference or which has "no work order" reference.

2. Inventory items in "stores" will be charged to the work order, so it is important that we continue to note the work order number on requisition cards for all parts removed from the stockroom.

3. While most of our inventory items already have been expensed and we cannot associate their cost with a particular job, accounting will continue to place some of these items in "stores" as they are ordered. Eventually, we will have many of our higher cost inventory items in "stores," with a unit price, so that we can properly assign their cost to individual work orders.

As a maintenance manager approves additional items to be added to stock, he completes a blank card showing item name, manufacturer's number or size, activity designation, estimated frequency of use, and critical outage code. This is sent to purchasing, and it will secure a best price and delivery. Then, accounting will assign a catalog number and bin number. The computer will then determine the economic order quantity, stock level, and order point for its own file, and issue ordering instructions, if appropriate. The computer then will store this information in its master inventory list and will add the item to the catalog the next time the catalog is printed. An interim supplement for stockroom use (see Figure 8-1) will be published immediately.

Fig. 8-1: Maintenance Inventory Addition Form

INITIATOR

    Item Name:____

    Manufacturer's Identification:______________________________________

    Using Activity Identification:______________________________________

    Estimated Use Frequency:________________________________/month

    Critical Outage:____

PURCHASING

    Price: \$_____________________________/each Delivery_____________

          \$___________________________/_____________________

ACCOUNTING

    Catalog Number:____

    Bin Number:____

DATA PROCESSING

    Economic Order Quantity (EOQ):___________________________

    Order Point:____

Fig. 8–2: Information Flow: Materials Control

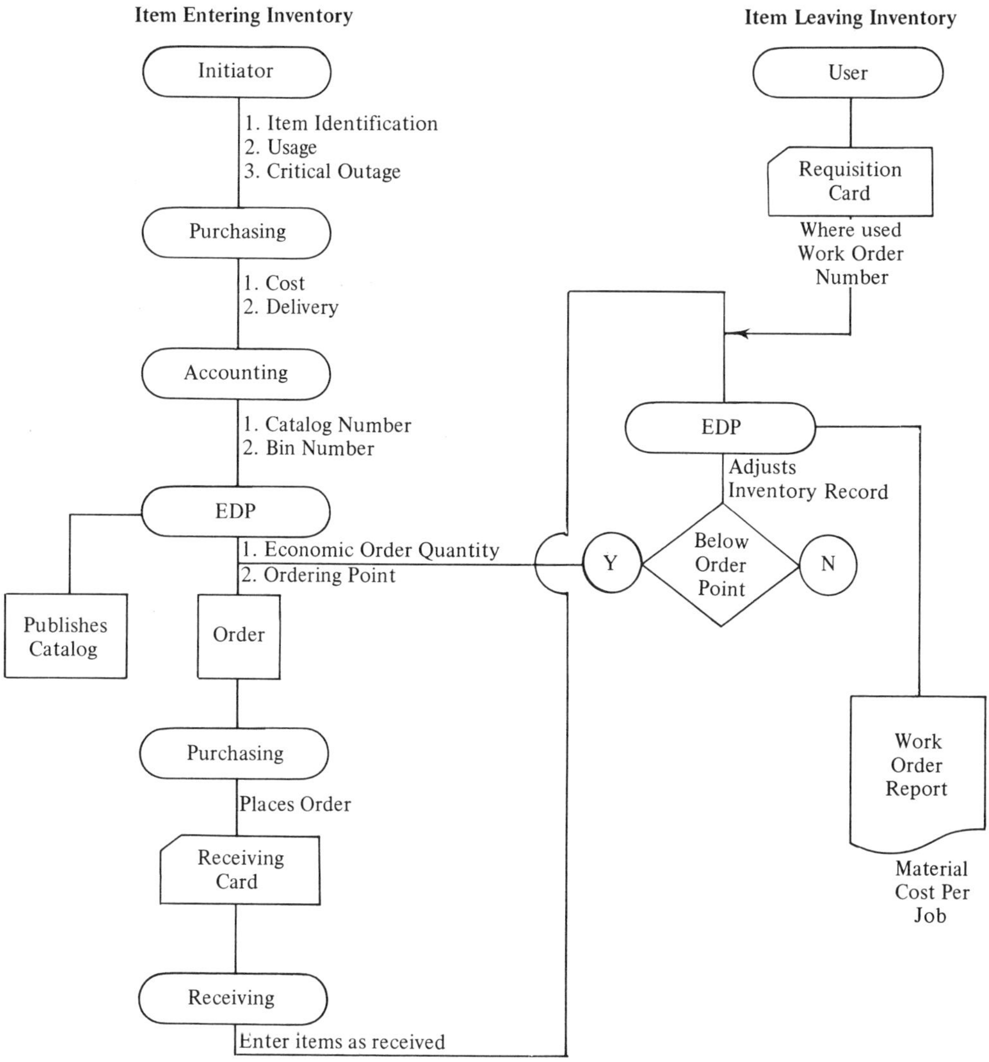

Item Entering Inventory   **Item Leaving Inventory**

IX. Lubrication

Lubrication is the area first explored for computer scheduling. Mobil Corporation's MI/DAC System has received a lot of attention recently and has been well exposed by Mobile Service Engineers. Generally, lubrication jobs that need to be performed at specific intervals, from daily to annually, are programmed into a master deck of cards. From this master, individual cards or a sheet schedule is printed at weekly or monthly intervals. This chapter will discuss the details of such a program.

Establishing a Lubrication Schedule

As with most computer programs, considerable effort must be expended to set up the original program. A good lubrication schedule requires the following information:

1. *A sequence number for each piece of equipment lubricated:* This is determined by an engineering study of the most efficient route to be taken by the oilers. The last digit is normally 0, or 5 and 0, to allow for insertion of additional equipment along the same route.
2. *Activity identification:* Designates the machine number and, also, the machine name.
3. *Part to be lubricated:* This may involve many parts on each machine and should specify such items as "worm gear," "feed bearings," "drive chain," etc. It is permissible to generalize only on such items as "miscellaneous–grease fittings" where the same grease is used and where there are fittings too numerous for their loca-

tions to be described accurately. We should itemize as many individual lube points as possible.

4. *Method of lubrication:* The means by which the lubricant is applied, examples of this category are "gun," "reservoir," "swab," and "cup."
5. *Lubricant:* This is the name of the lubricant used for that particular application.
6. *Lubrication frequency:* Daily, weekly, or monthly, etc., is specified for each application.

When all of this information is compiled, the computer arranges it in schedule form, according to the physical sequence of equipment. The computer balances all of the weekly, monthly, and longer interval items so that the oilers have about the same workload each day. For example, the first 20% of the weekly items will be scheduled on Monday, starting with the first item in sequence. The second 20% of weekly items will be on Tuesday, etc. Monthly and other long interval items are divided in the same way so that all items for one machine (other than daily) are scheduled on the same day of the week. Thus, on the third Wednesday of the fourth period (month), a machine may be scheduled for its daily work, two weekly items, one monthly item, and two quarterly items.

A schedule period is normally four weeks, regardless of how the months fall toward the end of the year. This allows for four separate schedules in a period of four weeks and, then, the cycle repeats. The items of duration longer than monthly are spread out among the four-week periods.

There are two forms of working schedule which can be derived from a master schedule. One is a series of printed cards, each one representing a separate lubrication item. These series, or packs of cards, with the printed scheduled date, are distributed to the oilers each day. The oiler checks each card as he completes that item and turns in completed cards at the end of the day. The second form has the computer printing a weekly sheet listing all items to be lubricated and the associated information (see Figure 9-1 for an example of the

Fig. 9–1: Format of Lubrication Schedule (Sample)

SANDUSKY FOUNDRY & MACHINE COMPANY
Schedule # 1, Week of _______________

Number	Machine Number	Machine Name	Part to be Lubricated	Method	Lube	M	T	W	T	F
0010	1122	Yoder Mill	Spindle drive gear case	Reservoir	DD	M				
			Main circulating system	Reservoir	Vac.HM	M				
			Miscellaneous oiled parts	Hand-cup	Vac.HM	M	T	W	T	F
			Slides & Ways	Gun	EP#1	M				
0020	1080	Drill Press	Spindle head main drives	Reservoir	Vac.HM	M				
			Elevating worm gear	Reservoir	DD	M				
			Elevating screw & column clips	Reservoir	DD	M				
			Miscellaneous oiled parts	Hand-cup	Vac.HM	M	T	W	T	F
			Positioning worm gear	Reservoir	DD	M				
			Shift head	Reservoir	DTE.26	M				
0030	1094	Drill Press	Hydraulic system	Reservoir	DTE.26	M				
			Drill spindles	Reservoir	AA	M				
			Lube systems (2)	Reservoir	Vac.#3	M				
			Miscellaneous grease fittings	Gun	EP#1	M				
			Index bearings	Reservoir	Vac.HM	M				
			Miscellaneous oiled parts	Hand-cup	Vac.HM	M				
0040	1085	Drill Press	Greased bearings	Gun	EP#1	M				
			Oiled bearings	Hand-cup	Vac.HM	M	T	W	T	F
			Feed worm drive	Reservoir	Vac.HM	M				
			Feed drive chain	Hand-cup	Vac.HM	M				
			Open gears	Swab	EP#1	M				
			Feed bearings	Hand-cup	Vac.HM	M				

format used). The oiler marks each item on the sheet as it is completed, in a way similar to the card method.

The schedule sheet is the preferred method from the standpoint of oiler efficiency. One can imagine the volume of cards involved in the individual system. The oiler would spend a great deal of his time sorting cards — and if he ever dropped them . . . ! The printed schedule sheet can be placed on a clipboard mounted on the lube cart so that documentation time spent by the oiler is minimized.

Items not completed can be noted at the end of the day and picked up the next day, or by another shift, or by whatever means common to the operation. As machines are added or relocated, or as lubrication requirements change, it is a simple matter to notify the computer section. A new card can be punched which reflects the change and then be placed in the master schedule in place of the old card.

X. Backlog

The backlog phase of computer maintenance is the real planning control of the maintenance operation. Through backlog reports, the maintenance manager can evaluate his manpower and plan for necessary additions or transfers. He can better determine which craft areas are capable of undertaking special projects and which projects should be given to outside contractors. He can determine which supervisory areas need extra help in pushing through the work and which estimators are accurate in their functions.

Establishing a Backlog Reporting System

The general interpretation of backlog is: all known future work requirements. There are two ways of defining and reporting this work. The first is all-inclusive, with preventive maintenance and routine scheduled work counted along with outstanding work requests. Such a report provides the total known hours of work to be done. The problem with including future scheduled work such as preventive maintenance is to know how far in the future to stop adding it into the total of outstanding man-hours.

Because our analysis deals primarily with trends and comparisons rather than with specific hours, the second, and preferred, way of reporting is to exclude preventive maintenance and other periodically scheduled work and to report only outstanding work requests. The monthly total of preventive maintenance and periodic man-hours will be somewhat constant and can be calculated easily and inserted whenever total man-hours are considered.

Thus, we are dealing only with individual work requests that are not urgent enough to be completed right away but are, instead, held for future scheduling. As noted earlier, each job received is estimated by maintenance department personnel before being sent to the computer section for processing, and hours for each craft code are separated on the written work request.

On jobs to be placed in backlog, the maintenance scheduler notes a "2" on the work request to indicate "backlog." A work request, noted "1," indicates an immediate requirement job. These latter requests often are accompanied by the completed handwritten work order and are received by the computer section for the purpose of inclusion in the work order report and any other applicable reports.

The work order receives a punch to indicate either "1" or "2." A "3" is used to identify preventive maintenance and periodic work and is written into the program when these work orders are printed. As a "backlog," or "2," punched job has its work order printed, the identifying information is added as another item in the computer backlog file. When a backlog job is finished and the work order card is sent back to the computer section for processing, the machine picks up this "2" punch and removes that job from the backlog file. We then have a continuous movement of jobs into and out of the backlog file.

The same process applies to preventive maintenance and periodic work. These jobs are added to the "preventive maintenance," or "3," file as they are printed, usually once each month.

The Backlog Report

A weekly backlog report is normal, but a printing of the backlog file can be done any day and can report the status, as of that day, of outstanding work yet to be done. (The format of this report is shown on Figure 10-1.) A report is also generated, usually monthly, showing the amount of preventive maintenance and periodic (Code 3) work not done as scheduled and still in the backlog.

Fig. 10–1: Format of Backlog Report

Craft	Date Received	Work Order Number	Estimated Time
Electrical	5-4-69	53280	10.0 (2)
	6-2-69	53474	24.0 (3)
	8-15-69	53623	42.0 (2)
	—	—	—
	—	—	—
			222.0
Plumbing	7-22-69	53556	16.0 (2)
	10-12-69	53941	24.0
	12-21-69	54220	8.0
	—	—	—
	—	—	—
			189.0

The backlog report is a useful tool to the scheduler. Broken down by craft, it lists each job by date received, starting with the oldest job. The scheduler can, for the most part, work right down the backlog list when scheduling work. There are some jobs which are known to be more urgent than others, and there are jobs for which there are special requests from initiators, but the backlog report is the basic guide. Without this report, experience tells us that it is too easy to lapse into a "Last In, First Out" (LIFO) scheduling process rather than the preferred "First In, First Out" (FIFO) method.

Some departments may want to add further priority categories to the work orders, but this writer's feeling is that this is superfluous, takes additional space on the card, and places the lowest priority jobs in a position where they may never get done. Urgent, same-day jobs are done right away, regardless, and never show up in the backlog. Work in backlog is of such varying priority that it is much easier and more equitable to schedule the work by date received.

The following describes a modified backlog reporting system where separate work orders are used. This system requires more handling than the one just described, but is presented here for the many maintenance departments operating with separate work orders. It has the advantage of flexibility over the single card system just described. (The backlog report generated is identical to that shown in Figure 10-1.)

Alternate Backlog Reporting System

The block diagram of the alternate backlog reporting system (Figure 10-2) describes the flow of work order file copies to the computer and back to facilitate the processing of two reports. This is the procedure:

1. The file copy of every work order is sent to the computer center immediately after it receives an estimated or standard time. In addition each work order will have the following information on it:
   a. account or identification number;
   b. work order (pre-printed) number;
   c. description.
      These are the different ways the work orders are originated:
      (1) *Emergency:* Foreman sends up blank work order with estimate; or, scheduler, upon receiving call from production, sends printed work order and file copy to foreman, who assigns estimate to file copy and returns to scheduler.
      (2) *Backlog:* Normal flow from scheduler to foreman and back to scheduler.
      (3) *Completed Work:* Night sheet; such a job is already done and, after the work order and file copy are typed, they are returned to the foreman who assigns an estimate of what the job should have taken.
      (4) *Preventive Maintenance Work:* All preventive maintenance work orders are printed one month in advance and sent to the computer center by the first day of that month.
2. The standard or estimated time is in the normal code:
   G = General Repair
   R = Machine Repair
   P = Plumbing-Heating
   B = Building Repair-Carpentry

Fig. 10–2: Alternate Backlog Reporting System

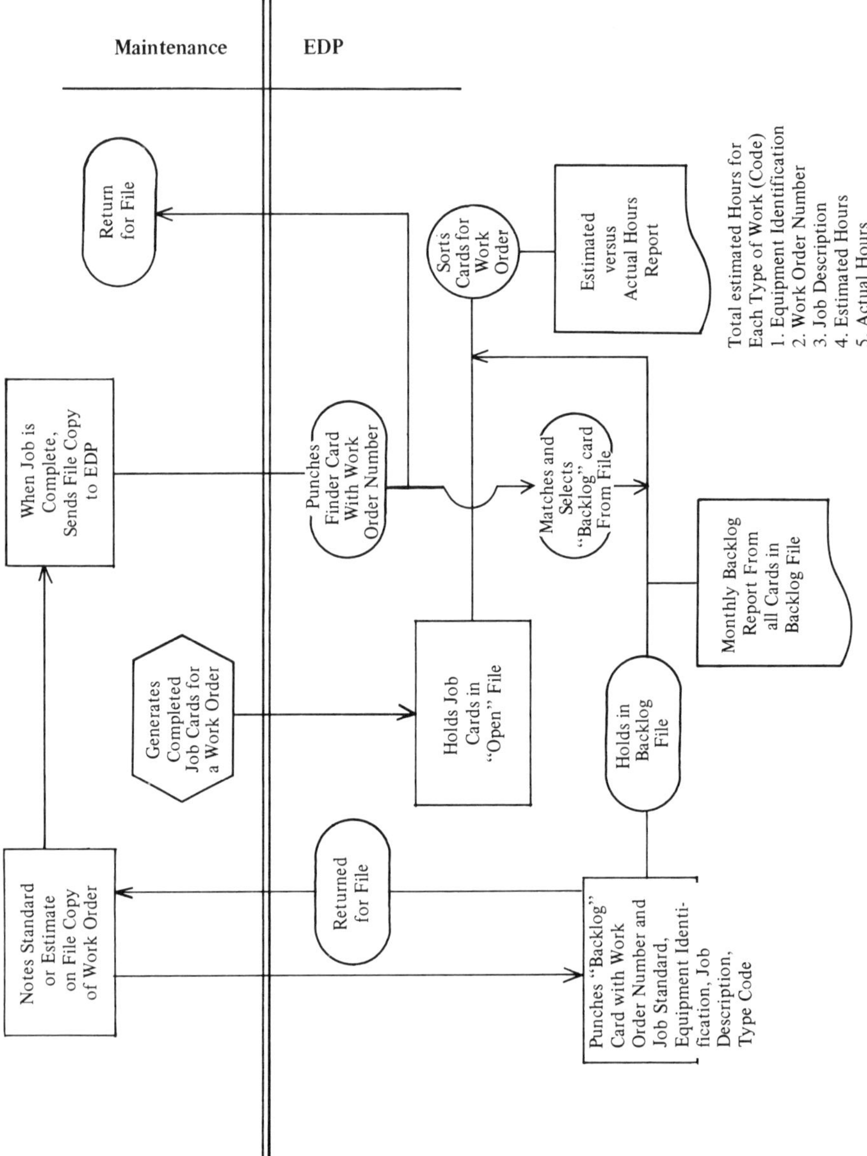

M = Machining
E = Electrical
V = Preventive Maintenance
(An example is "2 4P–8," which indicates a plumbing-heating job requiring two men for four hours, or a total of eight hours.)

3. The description is as brief as possible (limited to fifty spaces) and is used to allow easier identification of the work orders listed in the report. Simply underlining key words in the work required block, or writing a standard phrase, is required to tell the key punch operators what to use.

4. When the computer has taken the necessary information from the work order copy for its backlog card, the work order copy is returned to the maintenance clerk, who will do the following:
   a. Pair it with the work order and present it to the scheduler to place in backlog schedule; or,
   b. if it matches a completed work order, the scheduler will date stamp it to show completion and send it back to the computer center; or,
   c. if it matches a list of work orders which are in process, the scheduler will file the file copy in the appropriate rack pocket.

5. Actual times are generated on the work orders filled out each day by the maintenance men. These are collected by the computer until it is notified that the job is completed.

6. When the job has been completed, the maintenance clerk will date stamp the file copy of the work order and send it to computer processing. Night sheet and other jobs completed the same day will be date stamped and sent to the computer as complete, even though they have not previously been processed.

7. Computer processing, noting the date stamp on the file copy, collects the job tickets for that work order, adds them, and prints the total actual time as part of the monthly standard report. This re port will include identification number, work order number, description, estimated hours, and actual hours. At the same time, computer processing will remove the card for that work order from the backlog file. After they have used the file copy of the work

order, computer processing will return it to the maintenance clerk, who will pair it with the hard copy and then file them both.

8. As of the fifth day of each month, the computer prints a maintenance backlog report, using the backlog cards generated in step 4. This report shows total hours outstanding for each of the types of work.

Initially, many standard times are estimates. Having been assigned the task of compiling a list of oft-recurring jobs, the maintenance scheduler, with the assistance of the maintenance clerk, selects work orders and actual times taken from the monthly standards report labor report. The new standards report makes this job easier because it combines all the time on one report, regardless of whether or not it has taken place over a period of several months.

This list can be expanded as we become more familiar with the system. If we can standardize on the description for recurring jobs, the computer can collect them and calculate an average. Establishing standards is, necessarily, a long-term project and one which requires continual review.

It is through these standards, when properly presented to our maintenance men, that we begin to see savings result from more work output.

XI. Downtime

Dollars spent is one gauge of a maintenance department's effectiveness. Equipment downtime is another. Because there are many causes of machine downtime, such as operator absence, lack of material, and operating error, production reports of downtime often are not very meaningful to a maintenance manager. There must be a means to identify downtime which is attributable directly to maintenance.

We can develop a system which considers, in one direction, the effort of the production foreman to attribute downtime to maintenance, and the maintenance man's effort to reduce the record of maintenance downtime. Of course, our friend EDP comes into the picture by collecting data and publishing results.

An Effective Downtime System

A standard EDP card, often color-coded for easy identification, is kept in some quantity by each production area punch clock. There is a small, two-pocket card rack, with blank cards in one pocket and with the other pocket painted blazing red and marked "machines down."

Any time a machine goes down for maintenance in that area, the production foreman punches the time on a blank card, fills in the machine number, and places the card in the machine down pocket. When the equipment is repaired, the maintenance man removes the card, punches the time, fills in the work order number, and turns the card in to the maintenance department.

Someone in the administrative department section reviews the card, considers whether the machine is normally a one, two, or three shift machine, and calculates the chargeable downtime from the two clock-punched times on the card. He may, occasionally, have to check the production schedule to see how long a machine was scheduled, as in the case of downtime over a weekend. He also notes a class code to differentiate between kinds of downtime, according to the following:

Code 1:　Breakdown — non-scheduled.
Code 2:　Scheduled repairs — but at a time when there is *no open time* in the schedule.
Code 3:　Scheduled repairs — at a time when there *is open time* in the schedule.
Code 4:　Preventive maintenance inspections.

The card is then sent to the computer section where a monthly report is printed showing downtime by class and by machine with appropriate totals. The cards are stored and a special report can be generated at any time showing total downtime for any given machine or group of machines as far back as data are available. Figure 11-1 represents a section of a typical monthly report and a downtime card.

Historical Downtime

We must apply the same continuing analysis to downtime as we do to machine costs (see Chapter IV, *Cost Control*). With our monthly card file, it is easy to develop a periodic report every six months. This shows average of each machine for current six months, the last several six months' averages, and the total downtime to date (and time over which it occurred). Figure 11-2 depicts the format for the periodic report; included is a space for an assigned downtime cost per hour and the average annual downtime cost.

The information is easily stored in the EDP section on a single history card for each machine. Monthly cards are combined every six months and then discarded. The program calls for insertion of the latest six months' average, deletion of the oldest six months' average, and

Fig. 11-1: Machine Downtime Report and Card

S.R.	WORK ORD.	CLASS	HRS.	
1021	50861		1.3	*
			1.3	**
			1.3	***
1003	51174	1	2.5	*
1003	51182		2.2	*
			4.7	**
1004	51082		3.0	*
			3.0	**
1005	50999		3.6	*
			3.6	**
1021	50934		4.2	*
			4.2	**
1060	51045		4.3	*
			4.3	**
			19.8	***
1003	51071	2	.4	*
1003	51186		1.7	*
			2.1	**
1004	50940		.2	*
			.2	**
1005	51185		1.0	*
			1.0	**
1012	51157		.5	*
			.5	**
1016	51088		.2	*
			.2	**

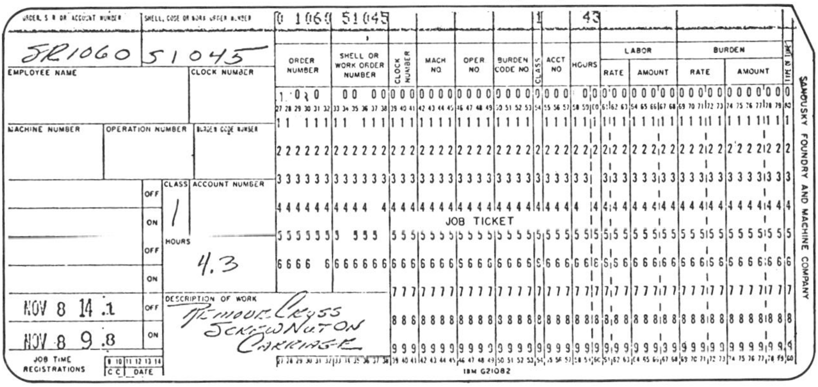

Nov. 1967

Fig. 11-2: Format of Historical Downtime Report

| Equipment Identification | Immediate Past Six Months Average Hours | | | | | Time of Total | Downtime Cost Per Hour | Average Annual Downtime Cost |
	Six Months	Twelve Months	Eighteen Months	Twenty-four Months	TOTAL			

creation of a new history card. Total hours and annual average cost are recalculated in the program.

General Downtime

Data processing equipment can, of course, develop all kinds of downtime combinations from the basic downtime input card. We should dwell for a time on the potential problems to be encountered in setting up the system. The very thoroughness of the coverage of this subject points to the need for maintenance managers to place prime importance on the documentation and subsequent minimization of downtime. Downtime is the name of the game and all preventive maintenance, record systems, tooling, and training efforts should be directed toward reducing a clearly defined number of downtime hours.

The intent of this section is to head off problems of definition for the maintenance manager in setting up a new downtime system. Every facility will have its own special problems, but the guide in the following "Areas of Preparation for a Downtime System" anticipates the general areas of controversy. Any system will most certainly have to be revised to some extent, but careful pre-planning will avoid major differences between production and management.

AREAS OF PREPARATION FOR A DOWNTIME SYSTEM

I. *RESPONSIBILITY*

For initiating card: production foreman

For closing out card: maintenance man

For reviewing card: maintenance manager, or nearest subordinate

II. *DEFINITION OF DOWNTIME*
1. For maintenance purposes only
2. Only when equipment was scheduled to operate otherwise
3. Not for operational downtime—tool changes, clean-up, etc.
4. (Optional separate category reported) For *maintenance* downtime at times other than when equipment is scheduled to operate

Establish many concrete examples of what is downtime and what is not. List each category and define, as follows:
   a. Breakdown maintenance
   b. Scheduled, but requiring rearrangement of production schedule
   c. Scheduled at a time when production schedule is open
   d. Preventive maintenance
   e. Maintenance at times when equipment would not have operated anyway (weekends, etc.)

III. *SYSTEM PRESENTATION*

System must be thoroughly explained and sold to:
1. Production management
2. Production foreman

Fig. 11–3: Information Flow: Downtime

Breakdown Occurs

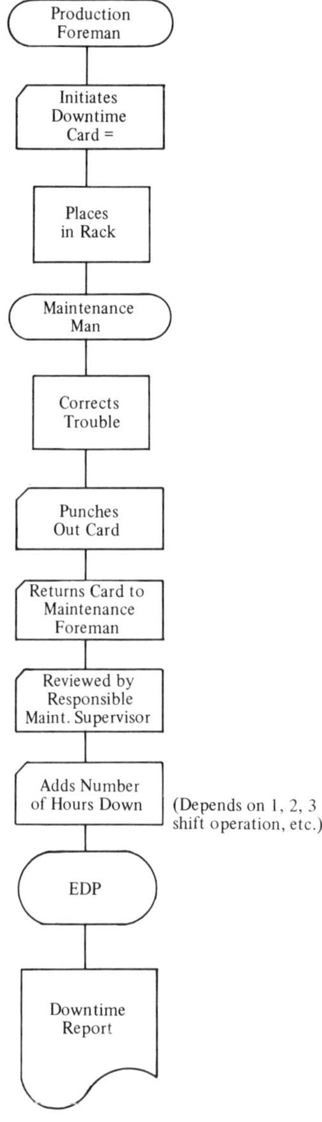

3. Maintenance supervision
4. Maintenance force

Post goal chart in maintenance department, showing weekly and monthly downtime hours.

A maintenance manager with a new downtime system has a bull by the horns; he is purporting to report the negative results of his department's efforts. His system can easily become an instrument for production's excuses but, at the same time, it will define, and show to be lesser, the problems of some machines' downtime exaggerated in the minds of maintenance and production alike.

One last point on downtime is the timing of introduction. Because it is the important index of maintenance effectiveness, it should be among the first new control programs introduced. It can then reflect the success or failure of all future changes or additions to a maintenance program. It is also an easy and straightforward data processing system and provides a good introduction to maintenance men to exception card reporting.

CASE STUDY VII: "MY DOWNTIME OR YOURS?"

Erie Machine and Tool Company was building a maintenance program. Jack Hill, Maintenance Manager, initiated a downtime system similar to the one described in the text. His basic concern was measuring maintenance effort to reduce lost machine time due to malfunctions. His exception card system was based on loss of *scheduled* machine time. If a lathe was down over a weekend, but not scheduled to run at that time, the weekend hours were subtracted from the elapsed time punched on the card.

He encountered two problems: 1) Inconsistency in initiating downtime cards by production foremen; and 2) definition of downtime. When the maintenance man failed to close out a downtime by punching out the card, it was pretty obvious by the card setting on the rack. While this caused some return trips to the job site, constant reminders by maintenance foremen to "punch out the card," and despite some confusion as to the actual time a job was completed, at least a downtime was recorded.

On the other hand, if the card was not initiated and the maintenance man and foreman let it slide by, that downtime was lost for record purposes. The production foremen's attitude followed the normal distribution curve very closely, with the standard deviation (68%) ranging from indifference to mild enthusiasm.

Compounding the foremen's attitude was Jack's second problem, definition. There are a number of "grey area" jobs that could be classified as normal machine operating service, such as changing turret lathes or chuck jaws or adjusting lathe carriage gibs. While these cause the equipment to be down, they are not really malfunctions. It is often difficult for the production foremen to draw the line between normal service downtime and maintenance downtime.

We could say that every time a maintenance man had to be called, it was maintenance downtime, but there are some minor legitimate malfunctions causing a few tenths downtime which are corrected by the operator. From the time Jack Hill's program was initiated and until it had been in operation for a couple of years, there was a suspicion in his mind that cards were not always initiated on smaller jobs.

Enter Carl Black, Superintendent, newly promoted to shop manager. He suddenly became aware of the possibility of using the two-year-old system as a means of justifying low shop production. The shop foremen were soon initiating downtime cards for every conceivable situation. Daily meetings were required to define specific down situations and, soon, the more common controversies were resolved.

In addition, Carl Black defined downtime as all time — on a seven-day basis — that a machine is not available for production, regardless of whether it is scheduled for use or not. Because this approach has merit for production planning purposes, a dual system was required.

This system incorporated an additional downtime code (5), for "machine down at unscheduled time." We now had the original downtime figures of last scheduled time which was a true production component and which was a bona fide measurement of maintenance efficiency and scheduling expertise. We also had a total elapsed hours down, which helped estimate future production capacities.

CASE STUDY VIII: THE HIDDEN COST

Ramjet Engineering, a medium-sized processor of exotic fuels, was experiencing difficulty in meeting shipments because of equipment breakdown. Rob Stanley, Plant Services Manager, had developed a pretty good maintenance program which minimized major breakdowns on critical equipment. Yet, production meetings became sheer "dread sessions" because of the production head's complaints of perpetual interruptions to the many processing lines.

There were numerous pieces of equipment with auxiliary assemblies. A fairly accurate maintenance cost was kept on each one, but a review of these did not reveal any outstanding offender. Each production chief had his own opinion as to which piece of equipment was his biggest problem, but that opinion was subject to change with that day's breakdown. Even the maintenance men and supervisors were at odds when discussing the machine which first should be replaced, redesigned, or rebuilt.

The answer, of course, was to go to the equipment itself. A simple exception card downtime reporting system was put into effect immediately. Each piece of definable equipment was included in the program. What took a while longer and much cooperation from production management and cost accounting, was a downtime cost per hour for each of the defined pieces of equipment.

While the available maintenance costs for each item provided a guide to those which should be included first in the downtime cost review, the total *downtime cost* for some equipment was completely *disproportional* to the *maintenance* cost. Some relatively insignificant item (an out-of-way pump, for example), when assigned a realistic figure of what its failure meant in terms of dollars, suddenly loomed all important. A large storage bin elevator, while an obvious headache to production and maintenance, actually caused a relatively low cost when inoperative.

The individual downtimes, while of short duration, became substantial downtime costs in the first few months of the system. The pump that, heretofore, brought the comment, "Oh, it needs repacking once in a while," was suddenly a prime contributor to downtime *cost*. A simple addition of a Viton packing, and a potential high cost of downtime was minimized.

With the same situation occurring throughout the plant, downtime costs were soon brought under control. A byproduct of the system, with the unexpected large downtime costs generated, was a top management decree for a complete equipment evaluation and replacement program. It has been obvious to the maintenance manager reading this narrative that it is the equipment which is generally old and worn that generates numerous small breakdowns.

The small plant maintenance manager may feel, because he is so intimately familiar with all of his equipment, that he doesn't need a system to tell him where his trouble spots are. It is undoubtedly true that he knows all about his biggest headaches, but does he really know what each is costing in terms of downtime dollars? And, more important, without this quantitative approach, can his top management know that replacing that grinder will pay for itself in downtime savings in less than a year?

Any good replacement model requires an input of present and expected downtime cost, operating efficiency, or similar parameter. While the new equipment must be evaluated on paper or from personal recommendations, it is very comforting for the maintenance manager to have factual cost information (maintenance *plus* downtime) when completing his replacement study.

XII. Training Control

Philosophy of Maintenance Training

Complexity of modern production equipment presents an all-too-obvious need for better skilled maintenance men. Alert companies are scrambling to keep even with training requirements. In this chapter, we will discuss a unique approach to control of maintenance training.

To fully understand the need for training control, let's talk about what we are really trying to accomplish. We have two basic maintenance training problems.

The first involves our experienced men who, if we have upgraded properly, have reached the top of their rate and possess a fairly high degree of skill. It is a comparatively simple task to seek out special OEM (original equipment manufacturer) and distributor training sessions for these people, pay their way, and trust that they receive qualified instruction — and that they absorb a sufficient amount of instruction to justify the expense! Experience tells us that such schools are excellent, and if the man is selected on the basis of his interest in the field, the schooling will be worthwhile. While this situation requires considerable effort on the part of maintenance management to find the schools, arrange admission, and balance training among the skilled people, it is not nearly as difficult a problem as that presented by the second maintenance problem, training newly hired, inexperienced personnel.

New maintenance personnel, while requiring a great amount of concentrated training effort, nevertheless present an opportunity for teaching the best techniques, without the handicap of previously acquired bad work habits. There are two distinct phases to the new man's learning process: technical schooling and on-the-job training.

Technical schooling can mean any one of several methods, including manufacturing and distributor schools, local adult education and technical school classes, and correspondence courses. While classroom work is generally preferred, the reputable correspondence schools can definitely fill needs from basic arithmetic up to advanced engineering.

On-the-job training is the more complex and difficult phase. We must teach proper maintenance techniques and we must ensure familiarization with equipment and knowledge of specific tasks. Techniques can only be learned from foremen, crew leaders, and fellow workers; and the rate of assimilation of these work methods can be related only to the interest of the man, his teacher, and the general learning atmosphere generated by maintenance management. Beyond encouraging this atmosphere of learning and cooperation, the maintenance manager is limited as to what he can do to control the technique learning process.

Unfortunately, many companies seem to rely on time, also, to take care of equipment familiarization and specific job training. If training is at all organized, it is set up on a calendar basis; that is, a new man spends an allotted time in different work areas with the hope that he will absorb knowledge of that area. This is not enough. There must be a formal system to insure that the trainee receives specific instruction in *each* element of work in the classification to which he is assigned.

Controlled Maintenance Training

This procedure requires an itemized listing of every job that the new man will be required to do. In most cases, these can be specific types of work, even on specific equipment, such as "Fill Niles lathe carriages with nitrogen." In other areas, the job element must be more general in nature, such as "repair air rammers." The manner in which these jobs are organized depends mainly on the job classifications and union restrictions.

A skill level designation can be assigned to each job. Completion of the training requirements for each job can be used as a guide for upgrading. For example, for a man to be upgraded from "maintenance man, grade B" to "maintenance man, grade A," he would have to have completed all the "B" level items and 50% of the "A" level items. To reach the top of "grade A," he must complete all the "grade A" items.

Figure 12-1 is an example of the elements used in a system with a "general maintenance" category as top classification. The elements are organized by trade for easy identification and for facilitating area training asignments. This system is also very useful in identifying training and experience deficiencies of long-time employees already at the top of their rate.

Training Control by EDP

We have described two phases of training—formal schools and on-the-job training — which must be efficiently planned and controlled to justify their expense. EDP can be the control method necessary to monitor the training received by each maintenance man.

The first step in setting up the control is to compile lists of training items required for each classification level. These lists should include the formal schools to be attended and each on-the-job training type of job. A color-coded card is punched for each item and a computer file of training requirements established which is keyed to a work order number for each item. This deck of cards is given to the scheduler, as are all other work order cards.

The scheduler schedules the men for training items, according to the department's general training plan. This training work order is the one actually used to account for the trainees' time on that item. In many cases, one day's work does not complete the requirements for that training item, so supplementary cards are used to report daily time. These cards (blank) are also color-coded and punched to identify them as training cards, so that the computer can log the time against that training item in the report for that trainee. When the foreman determines that the training is complete, he marks the completed date on the original training work order and, as with any completed work order, sends it up to the EDP section.

Formal schooling cards are pulled and returned to EDP for proc-

Fig. 12–1: Maintenance Department Skill Achievement Record

Sandusky Foundry and Machine Company General Maintenance

Name __________________________

Routine Maintenance	Level	Compl.	General Repair		Level	Compl.
Casting Machine Change	B		Cleaning Roll Chain-Sprocket		A	
Skimmers-Chisels	B		Pull Car Chain-Sprocket		A	
Clean Coolant Tanks	B		Overhead Doors		A	
Clean Dust Collector	B		Dust Bag Replacement	*	A	
Replace Coolant Hoses	B		Replace Way Wipers	*	A	
Repair Air Hoses	B		Replace Crane Cables	*	A	
Cut Skimmer Blocks	B					
Clean Coolant Filters-Tanks	B					
Steam Clean Molds	B		Replace Sand Mixer Floor	*	G	
			Casting Machine Oil Pumps		G	
			Casting Machine Mist Systems		G	
Conveyor Brushes	A		Drills Sprockets and Chain		G	
Adjust Sand Mixer Plows	A		Repair Air Rammers	*	G	
Build Up Spiders	A		Repair Coolant Pumps		G	
Clean Boring Coolant Filters-Roper	A		Replace Crane Rail Hook Bolts		G	
Adjust Packing-Coolant Pumps	A		Ind. Furnace Platforms, Locks		G	
Replace or Repair Water, Gas			Repair Crane Gearing		G	
Valves	A		Remove, Install Large Lathe			
Clean and Lubricate Cranes	A		Centers		G	
Fill Niles Carriages w/Nitrogen	A		Apply and Finish Devcon		G	
Fill 1028 Steadyrest	A		Replace Electrode Cables-2052 *		G	
Operate All Plant Cranes	A		Replace Electrode Cables-2053 *		G	
Simple Weld Repair	A					
			Ladle Gearing		S	
			Spray Car Valves, Regulator		S	
Install Mold Rings	G		Conveyor Drive		S	
Install Roller Tires	G		Spray Car Drive		S	
Drill Rail Change	G		Repair Drill Spindles		S	
			Welding, Repair and Fabrication		S	
Case Band Removal	G		Repair Crane Hook Blocks, Upper			
			Sheaves		S	
Case Band Installation	S		Adjust Gibs		S	

*General Job Element

Fig. 12-1: Skill Achievement Record (Continued)

Sandusky Foundry and Machine Company General Maintenance

Name ______________________________

Vehicle Repairs	Level	Compl.	Plumbing–Heating (Continued)		Level	Compl.
Daily Towmotor Checks	A		Clean and Inspect Heaters		A	
Lube and Oil Change	A					
Daily Hyster Check	A					
			Core Oven Valving	*	G	
			Inspect Steam Lines, Traps	*	G	
Generator Replacement	G		Drain Air Receiver Tank		G	
Starter Replacement	G		Blow-Out Ranarex Lines		G	
Brake Repair	G		Replace Sprinkler Heads	*	G	
			Repair Main Wash Basins		G	
			Drain, Overflow Water Tank		G	
			Replace Fire Extinguishers		G	
			Sprinkler Inspection	*	G	
Transmission Repair	S					
Clutch Repair	S					
Mast Repair	S					
Steering Repair	S		Remove, Repair Steam Heaters		S	
Grab Repair	S		Install Steam Heaters, Traps		S	
Engine Replacement	S		Install Gas Heaters		S	
Replace Lift, Travel Clutches	S		Remove, Repair Gas Heaters		S	
Repair Transmission	S		Sprinkler Inspection		S	
			Repair Steam Traps		S	
			Check, Clean Front Office Vacuum Pump System		S	
			Check, Clean Power House Vacuum Pump System		S	
			Clean Switchover Cooling Tower		S	
Plumbing–Heating						
Remove and Install Piping	B					
Install Copper Pipe and Tubing	A					

*General Job Element

Fig. 12–1: Skill Achievement Record (Continued)

Sandusky Foundry and Machine Company Electrical

Name ___________________________

Installation	Level	Compl.	Routine Maintenance (Cont'd)	Level	Compl.
New Lights	A		P.M. Inspection of		
			Small Lathes	G	
			Large Electronic Lathes	G	
New Motors, Alignment	G		Drills	G	
New Control Consoles	G		Cranes	G	
Motor-Generators-Alignment	G		Arc Furnaces	G	
			Induction Stations	G	
			Casting Machines	G	

Routine Maintenance

	Level	Compl.		Level	Compl.
Clean Air Filters	A				
Weekly Lubrication	A		*General Repairs*		
Grease Motors Properly	A				
Clean Capacitor Banks	A		Small Tools-Appliances	A	
Clean Crane Feedrails	A		Pyrometers	A	
Clean, Insp. Breakers,			Grinder Controls, Push Buttons	A	
Disconnect	A		Change Ind. Furnace and Station		
Clean, Lube Exhaust Fans	A		Straps	A	
Insp., Adjust Emergency Lite	A				
Check and Fill Batteries	A				
			Tear Down, Build-Up Motors	G	
			Align, Seat Furnace Contact		
			Blocks	G	
			Rebuild Furnace Contact Blocks	G	
			Rebuild Station Contact Blocks	G	

Fig. 12–1: Skill Achievement Record (Continued)

Sandusky Foundry and Machine Company Electrical

Name ________________________

Trouble-Shooting Failures	*Level*	*Compl.*	*Power House Operation*	*Level*	*Compl.*
Overhead Door Controls	A		Start Generators	A	
Gas Heater Controls	A		Start Compressors	A	
G.E. Office Unit Controls	A		Start Boilers	A	
			Check Compressor Safety		
			Thermocouples	A	
			Inspect Boiler Fire Eyes	A	
Core Oven Controls	G				
Heat Treat Oven Controls	G				
Mold Heating Oven Controls	G				
Boiler Controls	G				
Whiting Crane Controls	G				
MMM Crane Controls	G		*Power Distribution*		
Euclid Crane Controls	G				
Feed, Speed, Traverse Con-			Know Substation Arrangement		
troller on Standard Lathes	G		and Main Breaker Operation	A	
Electronic Controls - 1003	G		Know Physical and Circuit Lo-		
Electronic Controls - 1025-6-7	G		cations of all Secondary AC		
Electronic Controls - 1016			and Breakers and Disconnects	A	

essing as the trainee completes each assigned course. This can be done by anyone in the maintenance administration section generally responsible for training coordination.

We now have sufficient data to generate a training progress report (bi-weekly is a good interval) which allows us to monitor closely the progress of each person in a training status. The progress report tells how many hours were logged against individual items during that period, how much total time has been spent to date, and which items are still remaining. A report with the format shown in Figure 12-2 will keep us right on top of the training program.

This system eliminates a lot of time otherwise spent by the foreman marking progress sheets and otherwise noting training accomplishments. It makes training control more a scheduling function and frees the foreman to spend more time involved in actual training.

Fig. 12–2: Example of a Training Progress Control Report

Trainee	Item	Time Spent	Complete	Total On-The-Job Time Spent to Date	Areas with Items Still to be Completed
Pressler	Start Compressors	5.3			Routine Maintenance (4)
	Start Generators	6.0	X		General Repair (7)
	Start Boilers	11.5			Precision Repair (9)
	Blow Down Boilers	4.0	X		Vehicle Repair (0)
	- - - - - - - - - - - - - - -				Plumbing & Heating (0)
	- - - - - - - - - - - - - - -				
				138.0	Bearing Seminar (1)
	Fluid Power School		X		Wire Rope Session (1)
- - - - - -	- - - - - - - - - - - - - - -	- - - -	- -	- - - - -	- - - - - - - - - - - - - - - - - - - -
Cronk	- - - - - - - - - - - - - - -	- - - -			
	- - - - - - - - - - - - - - -				

Fig. 12–3: Information Flow: Training Control

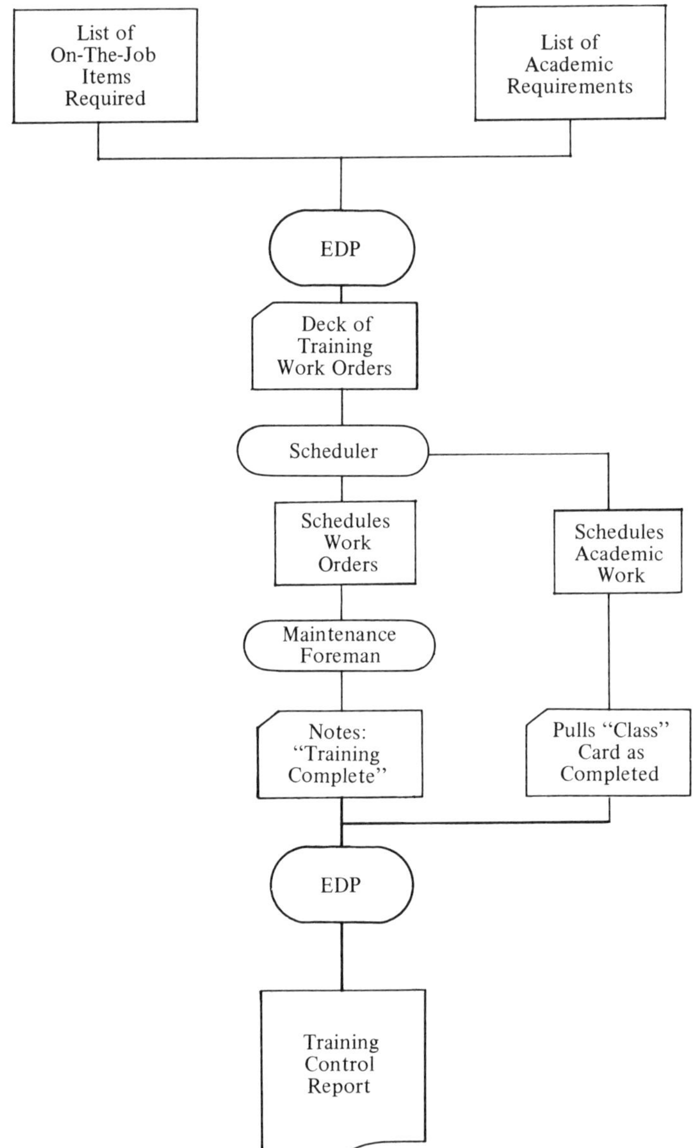

XIII. Equipment Maintenance Control and Replacement Planning

Part I: Vehicle Maintenance and Replacement

The importance of this field to a maintenance manager varies greatly from the small plant with two towmotors and a pick-up truck to the large plant with a fleet of vehicles and a fully equipped garage facility. The principles discussed herein, however, apply in either case.

Vehicle Data Required

A special computer input card is used which provides the following information:

1. Vehicle type identification
2. Vehicle make
3. Vehicle number (same type of number assigned to other kinds of plant equipment)
4. Odometer or hourmeter reading
5. Fuel and oil used
6. Work order number (This is pre-printed for different types of routine service work.)
7. Trouble code, action code, item code (Used in same manner as regular work orders, these are also pre-printed for some routine kinds of service work.)

This information is in addition to the normal name, clock number, and time spent information found on the regular work card. The emphasis on vehicle reporting is probably slanted a little toward recording fuel, parts, and service required for each truck rather than toward specific accountability for each man's time on each unit.

To reduce recording costs and to improve efficiency of the automotive mechanic, routine service time can be grouped for a number of vehicles. For instance, a man performing daily service for a number of towmotors would make out an individual card for each lift truck showing oil or gasoline used but, rather than figure his time spent on each truck, he would clip the cards together, with his total time on the top card. The timekeeping, or EDP section, figures an average time for each truck.

Vehicle repair jobs are handled in the same manner as any other repair except that they are done on the vehicle work order, which furnishes truck type, make, and mileage. Parts required are noted on material requisition cards, which are keyed to the job by the work order number.

Vehicle Maintenance Reports

Because vehicles are turned over faster than other plant equipment, we must monitor more closely their operating and maintenance costs. This need governs the types of reports we will want to generate.

Basic Cost Report. This monthly report lists each vehicle, mileage or hours, gasoline and oil consumed (each of these per hour or mile), repair parts cost, labor cost, and a total monthly cost. This monthly cost is shown as a mileage or hourly cost. A final column shows a cumulative cost for the last six months or year.

The vehicles are listed by similar models in order to provide a comparison between different types of vehicles and, also, between different makes of the same model.

Cost offenders are quickly spotted. For such offenders, we include a check figure in the program which is a cost limit established for each type of vehicle. When the "comparison test reads positive," we can print out the details of repair items for closer analysis. Of course, totals of fuel and oil consumption, parts and labor, and total costs, when compared to the previous period, provide an overview of vehicle maintenance trends (see Figure 13-1).

Fig. 13-1: Basic Vehicle Cost Report

Vehicle Identification	Mileage Hours	Gasoline Used	Gasoline Mile/Hour	Material Cost	Labor Cost	Total Monthly Cost	Monthly Cost/ Mile/Hour	Accumulated Cost for Past Six Months
867	310	110	2.8	$143.00	$46.00	$489.00	$1.58	$2380.00
868	260	92	2.8	62.00	32.00	364.00	1.41	1242.00
869	285	120	3.4	220.00	81.00	661.00	2.33	2691.00

Summation Report. This report lists each repair by item code and, within each item code, the action code. Vehicle number and cost are also included. This tells us whether our problems are concerned with distributors, tires, or masts, and if any one vehicle, or type of vehicle, is a habitual offender.

This report is best produced every other month. From it, we can determine parts specification changes for existing and newly purchased vehicles (see Figure 13-2).

Fig. 13–2: Major Item Replacement Data

Item	Action Code	Vehicle	Cost, Labor and Material
Distributor	2	867	$45.18
	2	1242	47.20
	2	943	38.22
	3	922	11.82
			$142.42
Tires	2	1041	—
	2	982	—
	8	—	—
		ETC.	

Usage Report. Produced every month, the usage report summarizes miles (or hours) between major component changes to determine intervals for these changes. The first step in this procedure is to determine an optimum replacement period for components. This is best established by history, with OEM recommendations as a guide. Even smaller plants, with few vehicles, have enough replacements to aid in an estimate, even if there are not enough to yield a statistically reliable average.

To begin, select the components you want to control, such as, tires, engine overhaul, transmission, steering, clutch, suspension etc. Each of these will have its own item code. This code along with the action code — "replace" or "overhaul" — is the key for the computer. The computer maintains a file for each selected component for each vehicle. This file shows the mileage (or hours) of each component replaced or overhauled. It can calculate at any time the average replacement interval for any vehicle or group of similar vehicles. This average figure is recalculated annually.

Once this average is established, the computer will scan the file for each component using a current mileage figure (always current from fuel and other work orders), subtracting the latest replacement mileage, and comparing the difference to the previously established optimum replacement interval (this interval figure is shortened slightly to allow for reporting and scheduling delay). If the comparison shows the optimum time to be surpassed, the component for the vehicle is printed in the report (see Figure 13-3). We can also program the com-

Fig. 13–3: Usage and Replacement Report

Vehicle Identification	Items Due Replacement/OH	Items Past Due Replacement/OH	Items Within 90% Replacement Period
867	Distributor	Transmission	
868	Engine Trans-mission		Tires
869	Mast Rollers		

puter to print the necessary work orders, in a way similar to the procedure used for work orders from the preventive maintenance schedule.

When the replacement is completed, the work order card with the appropriate item code-action code combination keys the computer to log that vehicle's current mileage figure in the file for that component.

As with most areas of computer applications, individual circumstance dictates specific reporting requirements. The above reports are representative of these requirements. The important point is to set up the thorough basic data inputs described herein. They are, again, by individual vehicle, mileage (or hours), fuel consumption and fuel consumption rates, total repair costs, and individual component replacement frequency and cost.

It may seem that we have gone a step further in controlling vehicle costs. The reason for this is that vehicle maintenance offers a greater sampling of like replaceable components which are adaptable to identifying codes and which are enough alike in performance for reliable failure data to be established. *The same component replacement approach can be applied to any group of equipment which meets these coding and frequency-of-failure criteria.*

Establishing Vehicle Replacement Intervals

This is a universal problem faced by maintenance and production managers — and by everyone driving his own automobile. Fortunately, at least for the industrial manager, appearance and prestige are not complicating factors. We can deal with our vehicle replacement program pretty much from a straight economical standpoint. A replacement schedule is established, based on the most economical possession or "turnover" interval. The time to replace is determined by the sum of the average cost of possession and the average repair costs over various intervals of time.

Establish Replacement Groups. This is done by checking the type and use of each vehicle and grouping them by similar operating conditions. For instance, 4,000# fork lifts used in the foundry would be in a group different from 2,000# fork lifts in the foundry and from 4,000# fork lifts used in the warehouse.

Determine Period of Replacement. We can program the computer to calculate replacement periods for us. We must provide the following information:

1. Repair Cost per Years Old (This is available from the basic cost report.)
2. Percentage Out of Commission Cost (This will vary, depending on the criticality of that particular vehicle group.)
3. Percent Depreciation per Years Old (This can be determined from vehicle suppliers and will, also, vary with vehicle group.)
4. Replacement Cost (This can be determined from vehicle suppliers and will vary with vehicle group. Both figure and depreciation also may vary from year to year, but it shouldn't be necessary to adjust them more than every two to three years.)

It probably isn't practical to take up valuable computer file space for this information, which is used only once a year, so the cost history of each vehicle is kept on cards which are stored by vehicle group. It is easy to change any of the above factors just by pulling a card and punching a new one.

Once the necessary information is secured, the method of investment theory used is a modified total average annual cost calculated over various time periods of ownership. There are two factors contributing to this cost.

The first is cost of replacement, or *cost of ownership:* This cost assumes initial possession and is based on the replacement cost in any given year, averaged over the number of years owned. The replacement cost, which rises sharply in the first few years due to initial depreciation, tends to stabilize in later years. This then contributes to a declining cost of replacement, because it is averaged over an increasing number of years possessed.

The second is cost to repair: This is the accumulated repair cost, up to a given year, average over the years possessed. Repair costs include labor and material.

Because out-of-commission time is a factor contributing in our decision, we must assign a cost in terms of total repair cost in order to consider this inconvenience. An arbitrary 25% might be an average for service vehicles in an industrial plant. In a cartage company, where the truck is primary production equipment, the out-of-commission rate would be considerably higher. This cost, in opposition to the decreasing "cost of replacement," will logically follow an upward trend.

The average replacement and repair costs are added to give an *average accumulated vehicle cost.* The age at which this average cost is lowest indicates the age at which each group should be replaced.

This replacement age will surely vary for each group as time progresses, due to model changes and usage. As a vehicle is replaced, we eliminate its cost data from that group and begin to include cost data for the new truck. Thus, we can update annual cost figures and provide a more current cost comparison.

The question arises: "Where in time sequence do I start to monitor costs in this way?" We have to assume that past cost data are available, but even if they aren't and the average accumulated cost continues down from the first vehicle age, you can assume that the optimum replacement point has not yet been reached. If the average accumulated cost rises from the first year (age) for which data are available, the optimum replacement year is that age or one earlier. Newly purchased vehicles will determine this when they establish a cost history.

The computer is now programmed to digest the necessary age and cost data and print out the average accumulated cost for each year of age for each group of vehicles. From this report, we select the optimum age at which the vehicle should be replaced. But what does the treasurer have to say about $30,000 worth of towmotors this year and none the next year?

Determine Replacement Schedule. Chances are that when the first study is complete, it will show a large percentage of existing vehicles have stayed around beyond their economic life. We can't replace them all this year, but we must have a starting point. The first step, then, is to assign a priority to those vehicles due for replacement, based on current repair costs.

Given a priority for those vehicles now due, plus the optimum age of replacement, year purchased, and current replacement cost, the computer determines the best possible replacement schedule with annual expenditures balanced. The computer must be given a limit of the number of years deviation from optimum for any given vehicle. This schedule will be recalculated each year considering any changes in optimum replacement year and purchase costs.

Lease or Buy Decision

The data from the basic cost report will support any comparative decision involving the leasing of vehicles. The average accumulated cost used in the replacement schedule is a more specific figure against which to compare costs of leasing. The out-of-commission factor should be extracted, however, because it will be a negative factor in both cases, though reflected in the cost to lease.

This study groups the vehicles by type and this may point to the leasing of some particularly high cost vehicle group. This approach must be studied carefully to insure that the average operating cost of the vehicle repair shop is not increased if the lessor provides maintenance service also.

Part II: Replacement Model Development and Application

At this point in our presentation, we deviate somewhat from our general approach to maintenance and computer and describe an example of how a statistical model is developed and used by the computer in a maintenance application. The pattern of solution development is the important aspect of this presentation. We describe herein a very thorough analysis of a problem with all qualitative aspects extruded into quantitative relationships, which the computer very easily converts to a dollar and cents answer.

Programmed Equipment Replacement Intervals Using Maintenance Cost Data

The subject of equipment replacement intervals has received considerable attention by proponents of scientific decision theory because it is a problem common to all industry and because it involves basic economic theory applicable to many business decisions. Readings encountered are usually centered on productive equipment with varying output rates to be compared.

However, basic in these models, as well as in those for utility equipment, are two main considerations, *increasing* operating and maintenance costs and *decreasing* average cost of investment as age is prolonged. The break-even point is adjusted by various interest rates, costs of capital, current values, and other financial factors. In addition are considerations for various efficiency and operating factors which are far more difficult to quantify and substantiate.

A common thread binds all this theory: The model must be adapted to individual situations.

Identification of Component Parts

This section of the development will describe the specific cost factors which must be considered. At this point in our model development process, we are only "brainstorming" the problem by listing all possible contributing variables. (The actual utilization of these factors is discussed in a later section.)

1. Annual repair costs for each towmotor (includes labor and material)
2. Replacement cost (the cost to replace each towmotor, based on new unit price and a depreciation factor; the consideration of salvage value)
3. Depreciation factor (used to determine replacement cost)
4. Out-of-commission factor
5. Operation cost (Is a new towmotor more efficient?)
6. Fuel costs (Do they vary with age of vehicle?)
7. Overhead costs (supervision, repair area, fringe benefits for mechanics, purchase order costs, etc.)
8. Loss of return on invested capital (affects replacement cost)
9. Tax consideration (Repair costs are expensed and result in a tax savings.)

Identification of Significant Environmental Factors

Other than the financial costs mentioned in the previous section, there are no objectionable features in replacing old equipment with new. Retraining operators may be a problem with very sophisticated machinery, but this is not a problem with lift truck operation.

There are, however, some considerations in favor of replacing the old equipment which, while not contributing to the basic monetary formula, can be assigned as low value variables favoring replacement.

Standardization. Trucks purchased can be standardized within the requirements of a particular job area. While there has been some trend toward smaller sized trucks, the trend is slow, and the basic mechanical truck remains fairly stable.

1. *Operators Advantage:* While these trucks are relatively simple to operate, they all have idiosyncrasies which can result in some loss of production time, since operators use different trucks at different times. The mechanical longevity of the trucks also improves with standardized operation and instructions.

2. *Maintenance Efficiency:* Certainly, automotive mechanics ben-

efit from improved knowledge and techniques they acquire from working on the same type of equipment.

3. *Parts Inventory Cost:* This is an area where standardization of equipment results in considerable money savings. Where we now stock several designs of the same part, for several different model towmotors, we could, by replacement and standardization, reduce inventory to just one type of each item.

Employee Morale. Any production manager can attest to the immeasurable positive effect on general working attitudes, cooperation, and communication in a work force given new, or even reasonably well-operating, equipment. The effect of replacing balky and sluggish lift trucks with new, smoothly operating ones is, obviously, a positive one.

Identification of Important Relationships

This section describes the framework into which our data should fit in order to consider the variables mentioned previously. There are three ideas which must be considered: use of individual lift trucks; grouping of similar use trucks; and base of comparison of maintenance cost data.

Use of Individual Lift Trucks. Consider the type of truck and the type of job it performs. Next, make sure that the best truck for that application will be used. It is this truck which will establish our replacement cost. Trucks are used for:

Metal hauling: barrel grabs, foundry
Metal hauling: fork lifts, foundry
Billet hauling: fork lifts, foundry
Chip hauling: fork lifts, shop
Heavy lifting: foundry
General use: shipping, building
Cat head storage: shop
Furnace loading: shop

Grouping of Similar Use Trucks. At this point in our problem development, it appears that, if we are to pursue our standardization theory, and, also, ease in handling data, we should establish the smallest number of truck use categories possible. Before deciding on the standard truck for each category and securing prices for a base replacement cost, a truck use survey form must be designed and distributed to operating superintendents. This assures that we consider the most suitable truck for present operating conditions. A form is used for each truck.

The results of the survey and empirical grouping produced the following categories of similar lift trucks. (Conditions are subject to change, which could produce alterations in the size of the trucks. Such a change requires only the insertion of another initial cost and modification of repair cost data. No such condition changes are indicated in the foreseeable future.)

1. Foundry barrel grabs: 4,000 pound
2. Foundry forks: 6,000 pound
3. Shop forks: 4,000 pound
4. Shipping forks: 4,000 pound
5. Large foundry forks: 3,000 pound

Base of Comparison of Maintenance Cost Data. Because we have such a variety of trucks, of many different ages, we should look carefully for a common means of comparison. Accumulated maintenance costs for each truck are not the complete answer because of the age difference. Average costs of all towmotors in a group are not satisfactory because they establish only one parameter.

Reviewing the basic problem definition directs us to a method involving costs at a specific age because we are looking for an age at which these costs, in combination with other factors, yield an optimum replacement age. Sufficient cost data for enough years of age are available in each truck group.

The method to be used for collecting the maintenance data is to accumulate annual labor and material costs for each truck at each year of age. If there are four trucks in a grouping, we will have four different cost figures for trucks at age "one year," four cost figures for age "two years," etc.

The fact that the cost figures for any particular age will have occurred in different calendar years tends to average out rising costs and any variations in plant production which would otherwise affect the maintenance costs to years of age relationship. Because all truck categories include trucks beyond the expected economical age of replacement, the actual data provide an economical replacement point without future costs having to be projected.

Data Collection and Statistical Analysis

Fortunately, accurate *maintenance cost* information is available for all the towmotors. Maintenance cost data are collected and arranged by towmotor group and by year of age within those groups. An average is taken for each year, and this figure is used in the final model application (see Figure 13-4).

Fig. 13–4: Repair Costs Versus Years of Age

Years of Age	Group B				Group C		
	861	860	863	(x) Average	858	857	(x) Average
1	–	–	–	–	339	427	383
2	–	–	890	890	472	433	453
3	–	–	–	–	620	570	595
4	566	–	–	566	551	607	579
5	342	–	–	342	541	682	611
6	433	476	–	455	852	690	771
7	321	200	–	261	912	1067	990
8	395	538	–	467	1370	1158	1264
9	897	999	–	948	1030	1244	1137
10	501	468	–	485	1763	1671	1717
11	421	850	–	636	1449	1596	1522
12	884	841	–	863	589	708	649
13	627	1353	–	990	2154	1341	1747
14	855	1328	–	1092	1856	1873	1864
15	957	1540	–	1249	–	2310	2310
16	683	2202	–	1443	–	1644	1644
17	846	1898	–	1372	–	–	–
18	533	1766	–	1150	–	–	–
19	1903	1715	–	1809	–	–	–
20	1935	1597	–	1766	–	–	–
21	–	2460	–	2460	–	–	–
22	–	2200	–	2200	–	–	–
23	–	–	–	–	–	–	–
24	–	–	–	–	–	–	–

The yearly average cost figures change each year as that year's costs are added. As mentioned above, the addition of current cost data to various years-of-age averages keep these averages statistically sound and sensitive to rising costs and changing production requirements.

Replacement Cost Data. These are obtained by securing firm quotes for the lift truck models selected to represent each group.

Depreciation Factor. For this analysis, the market value depreciation is used rather than the straight accounting department depreciation, because the towmotors in question are traded for the trucks which replace them, and their market values, or salvage values, at the time, contribute substantially to replacement costs. Market depreciation data are secured from lift truck distributors.

Out-of-Commission Factor. This factor represents the penalty imposed on production when a lift truck is out of commission for repairs. In a small fleet, where spare units are impractical, this downtime factor is considerable.

It is difficult to justify a figure in dollars for hours lost, so this factor is best expressed as a percentage of repair costs. A survey of the three operating superintendents results in remarkably close agreement on a factor of 25% of maintenance costs.

Fuel Costs. These can be eliminated from our problem. The difference in propane gas and oil consumption between new and old towmotors is insignificant. Most present trucks have been converted to propane gas and all new ones, also, will use this fuel. Electric trucks are not economical because of the long runs and steep ramps encountered in the normal operation.

Parts Inventory Cost. This is determined by reviewing the parts inventory catalog for identical items whose duplication could be eliminated by standardized replacement of towmotors. The dollar value of these items amounts to 6% of the total inventory. Material costs compared to total maintenance costs, yielded a figure of 35%. The parts inventory factor is, then, about 2% of total maintenance cost. This factor is eliminated from our model at a later date, when the standardization program is complete.

Other Factors. These do not require research and/or data collection and so are given as a group. These items are all very difficult to specify as quantitative factors, but, because they are recognized as positive arguments for towmotor replacement, we must assign, arbitrarily, some value to them, as a *personnel group:*

Operation Costs
Overhead Costs
Operators Advantage
Maintenance Efficiency
Employee Morale

A priori analysis indicates that this group of factors should be expressed as some sort of constant which increases with the age of the truck. In the final model, we analyze one truck at a time and deal with an average cost for one truck. These factors are not directly dependent on the magnitude of the average maintenance cost. For example, employee morale and operational savings, when considering one truck, improve to the same degree, regardless of the number of trucks in the group or the maintenance cost of the group.

A value of one dollar ($1), factored by the age of the truck squared, is assigned arbitrarily as the contribution for this *personnel group*.

Loss of Return on Invested Capital. This is based on a company-wide expectation of 7% on invested capital before taxes. This factor negative to replacement is calculated as an average rate over the term of the investment by adding the purchase price to the market value, dividing by two and multiplying by the 7% before taxes rate.

Tax Consideration. Since all operating costs can be expensed against profit, their effect must be reduced by 50%. This reduction is based on actual maintenance costs before the downtime factor is added.

Operational Definition of Variables

At this point, we have fully stated the problem, described all the component parts and contributing factors, and established a framework for data collection. While the development of a general model to resolve the problem has been in the background up to this point, it is now time to present and identify the specific contributing variables and constants which are used in the formulation of the model.

y = *Years of Age*

x = *Annual Repair Cost* (representing the average for one tow-motor in each group at age y)

P = *New Unit Price* (the distributor's best price for a new unit)

a = *Depreciation Factor* (used to modify the new unit price to determine the replacement cost)

b = *Out-of-Commission Factor* (a factor of 25% added to annual repair cost to reflect the downtime penalty)

c = *Part Inventory Savings* (a factor of 2% reduction of annual repair cost to reflect standardization of parts)

d = *Tax Consideration* (a factor of 50% applied against expensable maintenance costs)

e = *Personnel Group Factor* (a constant, with a value of $1)

f = *Loss of Return on Invested Capital* (reflects return that could be gained on money spent for new towmotors)

Formulation of Model

The most important basic problem requirement is *to determine which year is the most economical in which to replace the towmotors in each similar duty group.*

Average repair cost figured on the cumulative repair cost is the first variable in the model. The tax credit (d, or .50) is applied to the annual repair cost (x). The cumulative cost is divided by years of age (y) to determine average cost in that particular year.

The out-of-commission factor (b, or .25) is also applied to average repair cost.

A replacement cost ($a_y P$) is next to be considered. The new unit cost (P) is reduced by the depreciation factor (a_y), which reflects the decrease in trade-in value as years of age increase.

Cost of capital utilizes the expression for average investment, which is the sum of new price (P) and salvage value [$P(1 - a_y)$], divided by 2. This is then factored by the accepted return on investment percentage.

The parts inventory savings factor (c) is multiplied by annual repair cost.

The personnel group factor (e) has its greatest effect at later years of age. It is shown by the constant (e) times the square of the unit's age (y^2).

FINAL FORM OF MODEL

Where,

TAAC = Total Average Annual Cost
x = Annual Repair Cost
y = Years of Age
P = New Unit Price
a_y = Depreciation Factor (varies with y)
b = Out-of-Commission Factor (25% added to Annual Repair Cost to reflect downtime penalty)
c = Parts Inventory Savings (factor of 2% reduction of annual repair costs to reflect standardization of parts)
d = Tax Consideration (factor of 50% applied against expensable maintenance costs)
e = Personnel Group Factor ($1 as a factor of y^2 to reflect inefficiency of older units)
f = Return on investment standard (7%)

Then,

$$\text{TAAC} = \frac{\sum_{y=1}^{y} dx + bx + a_y P + f/2[P + P(1 - a_y)] - cx}{} + ey^2$$

$$= \frac{\sum_{y=1}^{y} .50x + .25x + a_y P + .035[P + P(1 - a_y)] - .02x}{} + 1.00y^2$$

$$= \frac{\sum_{y=1}^{y} .73x + a_y P + .035[P + P(1 - a_y)]}{} + y^2$$

Application of Model

A program was written for the computer and the data described in the preceding section were applied. Figure 13-5 summarizes the variables and constants. The results appear in the total average annual cost (TAAC) column for each towmotor group (see Figure 13-6).

From these data, we can easily select the year at which TAAC is lowest. A summary of the economic age for replacement for each group is shown as Figure 13-7.

Fig. 13–5: A Table of Variables and Constants

Years of Age (Y)	Depreciation Factor (A)	Towmotor Group	New Unit Price (P)
1	.45	A	$9,500
2	.50	B	7,000
3	.55	C	6,600
4	.60	D	7,000
5	.65	E	8,400
6	.67		
7	.69		
8	.71		
9	.73		
10	.75		
11	.78		
12	.81		
13	.84		b = .25
14	.87		c = .02
15	.90		d = .50
16	.91		e = $1.00
17	.92		f = .07
18	.93		
19	.94		
20	.95		
21	.95		
22	.96		
23	.96		
24	.97		
25	.97		

Development of Replacement Schedule

Knowing the economic life of each towmotor group, we have the basis for projection for each truck in a replacement schedule. The unknown factor is the starting point for each truck; in other words, which ones are to be replaced first. This choice is made simply by selecting the trucks which, considered individually, are highest above the economic age or which are carrying the highest total average annual cost above the optimum. Each truck which is past economic replacement age is run through the programmed model at current age and all trucks are listed in order of the difference between current cost and optimum cost, as shown in Figure 13-8. The remainder of trucks are listed in order of the number of years until economic replacement age.

We now have an *initial* replacement schedule. A further consideration for management is a policy to balance anticipated costs wherever

Fig. 13-6: Total Average Annual Cost (TAAC) for Each Group

Years of Age (Y)	Group A	Group B	Group C	Group D	Group E
1	5,067	–	3,609	–	–
2	3,108	2,263	2,132	–	–
3	2,506	–	1,679	1,489	–
4	2,336	1,417	1,454	1,246	1,438
5	2,218	1,264	1,328	1,116	1,338
6	2,148	1,146	1,237	1,017	1,193
7	1,980	1,047	1,200	938	1,094
8	1,857	997	1,202	893	1,014
9	1,794	1,002	1,199	965	964
10	1,809	978	1,244	931	939
11	1,820	980	1,280	966	959
12	1,803	1,001	1,262	972	1,000
13	1,861	1,031	1,313	969	1,015
14	1,883	1,068	1,369	971	1,035
15	–	1,113	1,445	998	1,129
16	–	1,158	1,479	1,021	1,157
17	–	1,201	–	1,056	1,192
18	–	1,236	–	1,069	–
19	–	1,298	–	1,092	–
20	–	1,358	–	1,116	–
21	–	1,439	–	1,166	–
22	–	1,513	–	1,205	–
23	–	–	–	–	–
24	–	–	–	–	–
25	–	–	–	–	–

possible. This means spreading out purchases so that too many will not occur in certain years. Fortunately, the initial replacement schedule fits this requirement pretty well.

In fitting the original replacement schedule and in planning subsequent replacement cycles, the decision maker must set a limit on how far he will alter the economic replacement age of any given truck. In this case, the limit is two years before or after the optimum age. There is always a choice involved between two or more trucks which fall due

Fig. 13-7: Economical Age of Replacement for Each Group

Group A:	Foundry Barrel Grabs	=	9
Group B:	Foundry Forks	=	10
Group C:	Shop Forks	=	9
Group D:	Shipping Forks	–	8
Group E:	Large Foundry Forks	=	10

Fig. 13–8: Order of Replacement of Present Lift Trucks

Truck	Age	Economic Age	Optimum Average Cost (TAAC)	TAAC at Present Age	Difference
860	22	10	978	1,513	535
861	20	10	978	1,358	380
859	22	8	893	1,205	312
857	16	9	1,199	1,479	280
864	17	10	939	1,192	253
862	16	10	939	1,157	218
855	19	8	893	1,092	199
858	14	9	1,199	1,369	170
856	14	9	1,794	1,883	89
866	11	9	1,794	1,820	26
867	11	9	1,794	1,820	26
868	6	9	—	Decreasing	—
863	2	10	—	Decreasing	—
869	1	9	—	Decreasing	—

for replacement in the same year. The choice of which one to move, obviously, is determined by which one will generate the least cost above optimum.

The number of trucks which we can expect to replace in any year should be computed before the master replacement schedule is finished. This figure is derived by multiplying the number of trucks in each replacement group by the economic age in each group; totaling these figures and dividing their sum by the total number of trucks to determine the average replacement age. Then, the total number of trucks is divided by the average replacement age to determine the ideal number to be replaced each year. The calculation follows:

$$\text{Group A:} \quad 5 \times 9 \ = 45$$
$$\text{Group B:} \quad 3 \times 10 = 30$$
$$\text{Group C:} \quad 2 \times 9 \ = 18$$
$$\text{Group D:} \quad 2 \times 8 \ = 16$$
$$\text{Group E:} \quad 2 \times 10 = 20$$
$$\overline{129}$$

$$129 \div 14 \ = 9.2 \ (\text{average replacement age})$$
$$14 \ \div 9.2 = 1.5 \ (\text{number replaced each year})$$

Fig. 13–9: A Final Replacement Schedule

Original Truck Number	Economic Replacement Age	1968	1969	1970	1971	1972	1973	1974	1975	1976	1977	1978	1979	1980	1981	1982	1983	1984	
860	10	7000										7000							
861	10	7000										7000							
859	8		7000								7000								
857	9		6600								6600								
864	10			8400										8400					
862	10			8400										8400					
855	8				7000								7000						
858	9				6600								6600						
856	9					9500									9500				
866	9					9500									9500				
867	9						9500									9500			
868	9							9500									9500		
863	10								7000										7000
869	9									9500								9500	
Annual Expenditure		14000	13600	16800	13600	19000	9500	9500	7000	9500	13600	14000	13600	16800	19000	9500	9500	9500	7000

We now know about what spacing to expect in expanding the replacement chart. With this background, we can start to construct our replacement chart.

First, set up a calendar matrix with years across the top and truck types listed vertically in order of replacement. Lay out and initial schedule, balancing costs based somewhat on the average number of trucks replaced per year.

A very important point should be considered now. The majority of trucks are overdue replacements in the initial year of replacement scheduling. A study of other replacement programs suggests that this is the case in most lift truck fleets! Therefore, we want to replace them just as fast as possible. Our initial cycle, then, will be somewhat compressed and not typical of later cycles.

The next step is to mark off the economic life from the initial replacement year for each truck. It is very unlikely that this cycle will balance out, so some of the trucks will have to be moved within the restriction of plus or minus two years. A final schedule is shown as Figure 13-9.

It is readily apparent that this procedure can be repeated annually or bi-annually and adjustments made to reflect any radical changes in operating conditions or replacement costs. As mentioned previously, these calculations are simple for our computer. Once the program is written, other replacement schedules can be calculated. The advantage is in being able to work with large quantities of equipment where manual calculations would be very burdensome.

XIV. Lighting

Tube and Lamp Replacement Intervals

Because of continued new development, lighting is becoming an increasingly important phase of plant engineering and maintenance. As plants become more elaborately lighted — and windowless building construction demands this — maintenance efforts must be increased correspondingly.

There are three phases of lighting maintenance which must be considered as contributing to total cost: (1) lighting inspections; (2) tube replacement and fixture repair labor; and (3) tube and bulb costs.

Lighting inspections are required at frequent intervals if the plant is on an individual lamp replacement schedule. If group re-lamping is used, the inspection intervals can be lengthened somewhat. In any event, the inspection and replacement of lamps should be done on a regularly scheduled basis. Any replacements are made at inspection, unless the light is a very critical one or if an offensive ballast must be replaced. This method, in opposition to dispatching someone to replace bulbs daily, has, in one instance, saved about $2500 per year. In this case the inspection of office lights is done at 11:00 P.M., just before the cleaning ladies are finished, so that lamps that have been in operation all day can be observed.

The major cost in lighting is bulb and tube replacement labor. This fact is the variable which makes practical the application of EDP to our lighting problem. The replacement decision involves the questions of (1) group or individual re-lamping and (2) how often to re-lamp (i.e., at what percent replacement of bulbs do we completely re-lamp?).

The biggest disadvantage of individual replacement is the start and stop time involved for every bulb replacement. Punching on and off the job often costs more than the tube.

In addition, most plants have a fixture cleaning program which they contract or do themselves. Cleaning involves elevating to the fixture, removing the cover, and then removing the tubes. Obviously, replacing the old tube with the new one is a minor addition to this procedure.

A logical and commonly accepted procedure is to replace all tubes and save a percentage (20%, for example) of the best appearing tubes. The degree of discoloration is an acceptable indicator of tube condition. Such discolored tubes are used as replacements and, when they are consumed, it is time for complete re-lamping. Theoretically, there is a break-even point where the incremental cost of individual replacements accelerates beyond the average cost of total re-lamping.

Enter the computer. While the mathematics are not terribly complicated, it would serve no purpose to explore them because there are programs already written which apply in most instances.

Computational services are offered by the major lamp manufacturers through their distributors. A lamp specialist visits the plant and collects data, including the number of each lamp type, daily hours used, and replacement labor costs. This information, along with bulb and tube costs, is presented to a central computer, and the EDP results indicate what type of lamp is best for the application, whether group re-lamping should be used, and, if so, how often.

Increasing Tube Life

Regardless of the optimum replacement schedule used, tube life is a major factor in cost savings. The following fact schedule was developed by the writer as a basis from which to issue on and off interval directions. The basic premise is that frequent startings shorten tube life to an even greater extent than continuous burning. While a computer was not used in this solution, it could be adapted for computer use in a plant with many different usage areas.

We used 817 fluorescent tubes in 1966, at an average of $0.79, or $645 total. This is relatively small when compared to the estimated $4.00 per tube replacement labor cost. A study was made to increase tube life.

A. Using the above figures and 7500 hours' average life, a tube is worth $.00064/hour in replacement cost. At $.0125/KWH, a common 40-watt tube costs $0.0005 per hour to operate.
B. A start reduces tube life as much as a few hours' burning time. Using manufactures' figures of: 100% life for 3 hours/start; 125% life for 6 hours/start; and 160% life for 12 hours/start, a curve was drawn from which tube life hours could be secured for any number hours per start (see Figure 14-1).

Hours Off	Hours On	Hours Start	Hours Life	Days Life
0	16	16	12,900	806
1	15	7½	10,100	673
2	14	7	9,900	707
3	13	6½	9,600	738
4	12	6	9,400	783
5	11	5½	9,100	827

C. Based on an average sixteen operating hours per day (8:00 A.M to 12:00 midnight), life spans were determined for different length periods of time during which lights were out (see Figure 14-2).
D. Making a comparison between the continuous burning life of 806 days, the tube life cost for each period of lights off was calculated, using sixteen hours for each day lost and our previously calculated replacement cost per hour.

> Example: For lights off one (1) hour:
>
> $$\begin{array}{r} 806 \text{ days — on full time} \\ -\,673 \text{ days — off one hour per day} \\ \hline 133 \\ \times\quad 16 \text{ hours} \\ \hline 2128 \text{ hours} \\ \times\ \$.00064 \\ \hline =\ \$\ 1.36 \text{ lost in tube life.} \end{array}$$

E. On the other side of the ledger, power consumption cost was calculated for each period of lights out, using the 806 days possible with continuous burning.

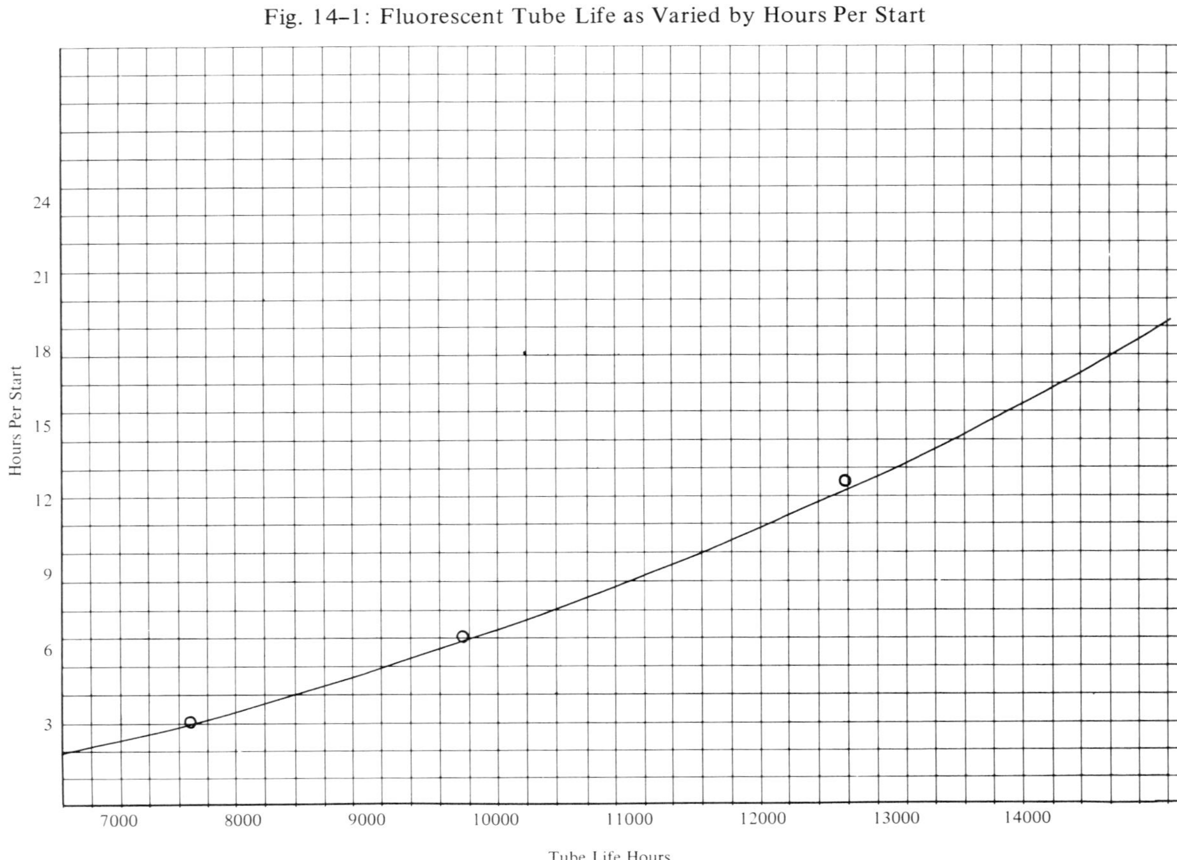
Fig. 14-1: Fluorescent Tube Life as Varied by Hours Per Start
Hours Per Start
24
21
18
15
12
9
6
3
7000
8000
9000
10000
11000
12000
13000
14000
Tube Life Hours

Fig. 14-2: Life of Fluorescent Tubes for Different Daily Usage Times and Different Hours Per Start

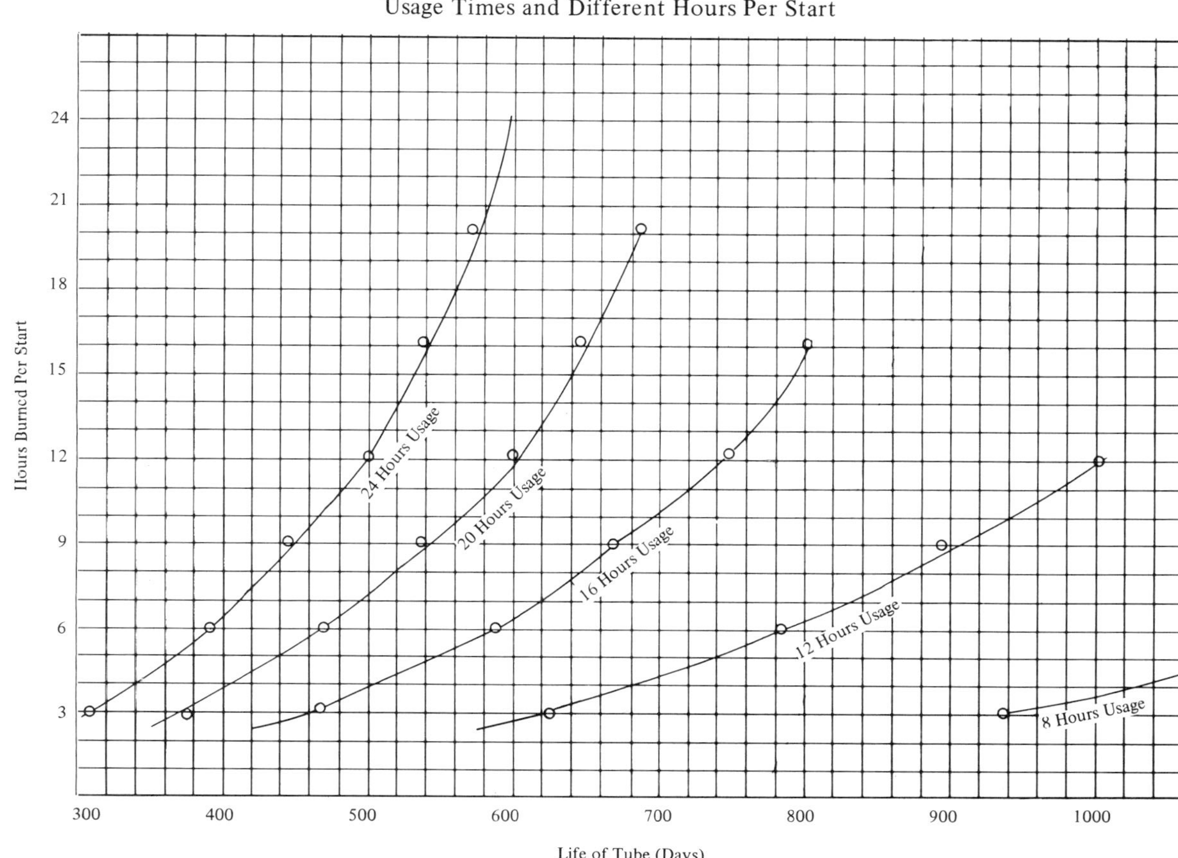

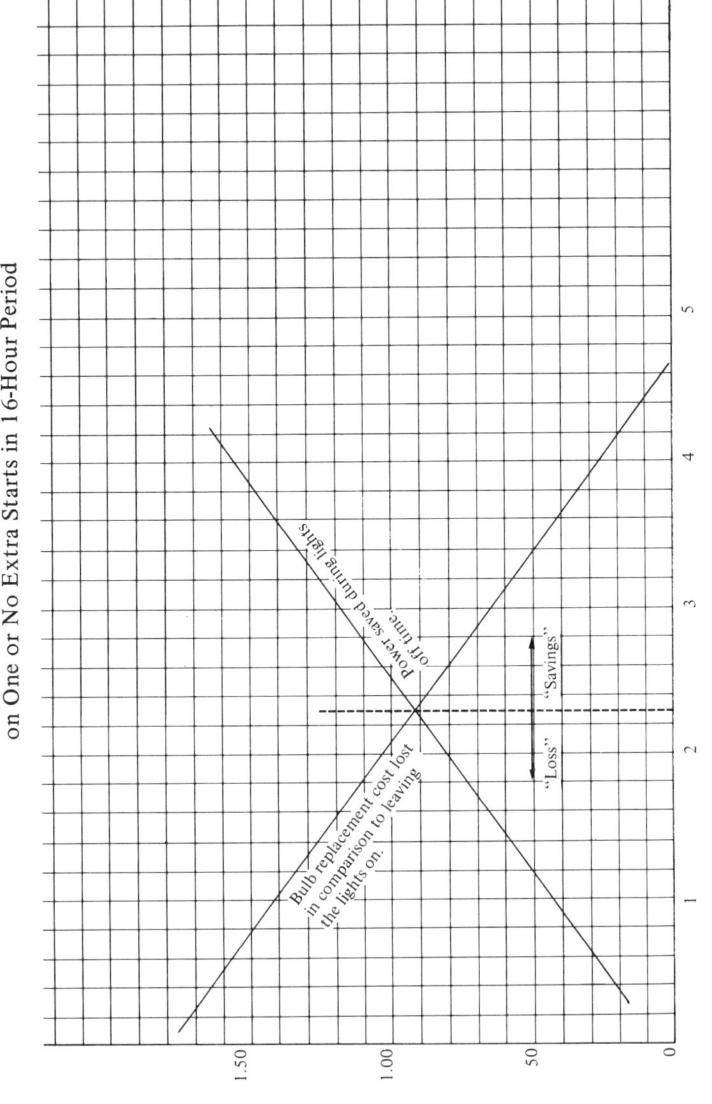

Fig. 14–3: Cost Comparison Between Turning Lights Out and Restarting, and Leaving Lights On. Per Tube Cost for Life of Tube Based on One or No Extra Starts in 16-Hour Period

Example: For light off one (1) hour:

$$\begin{array}{r} 1 \text{ hour per day saved} \\ \times\ 806 \text{ days} \\ \hline 806 \text{ hours} \\ \times\ \$.0005 \\ \hline \$\ .40 \text{ saved in tube life.} \end{array}$$

F. A graph of these costs and savings shows an intersection between two and three hours lights off as most economical (see Figure 14-3).

Savings in the Life of the Tube for Turning Lights
off for X Lengths of Time in a 16-Hour Period

Lights Off For	Power Cost Saved	Tube Life Lost	Net Savings
1 hour	$ .40	$-1.36	$-.96
2 hours	.81	-1.02	-.21
3 hours	1.21	- .70	.51
4 hours	1.51	- .24	1.27
5 hours	2.02	+ .23	2.25

The rule, "Turn lights off if they will stay off for more than three hours, otherwise leave them on," then, can be distributed to all personnel concerned with starting lights.

XV. Overtime Balancing

Overtime balancing is a relatively simple procedure, but one that pays big dividends in reduction of bad feeling and union grievances.

That any hourly worker is protective of his overtime is a fact recognized by a supervisor anywhere at any level. A manager had better be prepared to document the hours allowed to men of equal ability. The mere existence of such a record will erase doubts in most minds and convince workers that management is making every effort to allocate this overtime equitably.

A report is generated weekly from the labor reporting card, which lists each man by name and craft group. Opposite each name is the number of time-and-a-half hours, the number of doubletime hours, and the number of premium dollars for that week. Also listed are the hours accumulated in these categories for the year to date.

This report has been invaluable at weekly weekend work planning sessions (see Figure 15-1).

Fig. 15-1: A Maintenance Premium Hour Report

Week Ending July 6, 1969

| | | Hours | | | | | | Dollars | |
| | | Weekly | | | Accumulated | | | | |
Clock	Name	½ Rate	D.T.Rate	Totals	½ Rate	D.T.Rate	Totals	Weekly Total	Accumulated Total
4	L.L. Coe	.5		.5	256.0	7.14	327.4	$ .87	$696.76
47	A.F. Lortcher, Jr.				211.0	152.0	363.0		937.29
73	F.F. Weis				72.2	8.0	80.2		172.09
118	R.K. Lamarca				204.6	67.3	271.9		592.12
135	J. Leto				227.4	55.5	282.9		702.28
141	B.B. Haggerty	1.6	3.5	5.1	303.0	78.7	381.7	15.12	804.81
143	R.L. Yontz*	1.2		1.2	186.5	72.4	258.9	2.09	578.52
149	E.E. Oney	2.9	2.0	4.9	254.4	89.9	344.3	13.39	817.39
154	J. Teasel				222.7	8.0	230.7		416.55
182	J. Fedlam	3.0		3.0	261.2	70.0	331.2	5.24	701.19
46	J.J. Babcock, Jr.		.4	.4	222.0	91.3	313.3	1.46	735.17
72	J.E. Bergman				204.1	143.3	347.4		824.38
122	D.H. Wiesenauer				224.5	96.1	320.6		785.41
126	D.E. Davis				168.8	83.5	252.3		608.42
401	A.E. Fox	3.1	1.4	4.5	210.2	100.9	311.1	10.41	719.12
76	C. Salyer				182.0	79.3	261.3		546.66
81	K.I. Riccelli				139.0	39.0	178.0		316.82
194	J.M. Callan	1.5	9.1	10.6	251.9	53.2	305.1	30.83	546.66
422	E.A. Firby				214.9	22.0	236.9		415.55
		13.8	16.4	30.2	4,016.4	1,381.8	5,398.2	$79.41	$11,917.19

*Denotes Termination

XVI. The Total Program

This chapter summarizes the major points that a maintenance manager should consider when initiating a computerized maintenance program or expanding an existing program.

Individuality of Application

The material just presented is somewhat general in nature and purposely so. The maintenance manager must recognize that his operation is unique and any program he develops must be tailored exactly to his needs. New ideas can be made operative and relevant decisions can be forced by a computerized program, but its general intent must support company policy.

The extent of the program is largely determined by the size of the operation and the availability of computer and programming time. There is practically no limit to computer applications in a multi-plant operation with a large EDP staff. A small company which leases computer time must evaluate the cost advantage more carefully. This is not to suggest that a large corporation does not weigh cost advantages, but, rather, that they will see a greater "volume" of cost savings result from the same "fixed" programming cost which must be paid by the small concern. Keypunching and processing cost is directly proportional to the data volume and is, therefore, proportional to the cost savings involved.

The criticality of maintenance in a particular operation also affects the extent of its maintenance control program. Certain process industries, where any breakdown is crucial, are more willing to buy sophisticated maintenance controls than multiple product job shops, where breakdowns do not present problems of quite such magnitude.

The Sell: Necessary?

Top management, fortunately, is increasingly more willing to accept computerized programs. Those that were hurt initially by attempting too much too fast have settled down to a more realistic approach. Improved technology and cost structures have encouraged even the most conservative businessman to venture into seeking computerized assistance for his programs. Business publications and trade journals have been contributing subtle direction to management to modernize maintenance approaches for some time.

If selling a program is necessary — and, at least, presenting the program is — start with a large current problem. Show specific cost savings in solving the problem. Don't clutter up the presentation with a lot of detailed projects. Some mention should be made of other possibilities, but the *sell* should be based on a solution to a major, current problem.

This approach, also, applies to the implementation of programs. Don't attempt to tackle too much at first. Firmly set up the basic labor input reporting system and allow the maintenance men and all concerned to become completely familiar with it before adding the many intricate variations possible. These will come easily once that "long first step" is taken.

EDP = Assistant

Bear in mind that EDP (and the computer) is an *assistant* to the maintenance department. It does not run the operation. It will do almost anything it is asked in the way of compiling, processing, and presenting data. If a program or a report is not completely satisfactory, don't bend the operation to satisfy a requirement of the report at the expense of some other phase of the operation. Periodically review all reports to insure they still strike at the heart of current problems. Don't be afraid to discontinue or alter reports and procedures that no longer contribute substantially to the solution of current control problems. The greatest enemy of electronic data processing today is the accumulation of meaningless run files.

EDP is a tool. The maintenance manager must sell his maintenance men, himself, and his top management on the fact that it *is* a tool which, if used correctly, will provide a more interesting and a more profitable operation.

Bibliography

"ADP Can Help Manage Maintenance, Too," *Financial Executive*. April, 1963.

Carl, J. H. "Computer System Puts Squeeze on High Maintenance Costs," *Iron Age*. October 24, 1963.

Cash, Robert G. "Computerized Control of Maintenance," *Techniques of Plant Engineering and Maintenance,* Vol. XVI. New York: Clapp and Poliak, Inc., 1965, p. 21.

"Cost Control Productivity Without Paperwork," *Factory*. February, 1966.

Costales, R. R. "Adapting Data Processing to Preventive Maintenance," *Techniques of Plant Engineering and Maintenance,* Vol. XV. New York: Clapp and Poliak, 1964, p. 78.

Damm, Edward. "Costs Down, Efficiency Up When a Computer Controls Maintenance," *Maintenance*. October, 1965.

Dryden, L. S. "Computer Keeps Careful Check on Vehicle Maintenance Costs," *Plant Engineering*. August, 1967, p. 123.

"Experience Schedules Lubrication," *Maintenance*. October, 1966.

Goudreau, A. G. "Oil When Ready With EDP," *Iron Age*. December 24, 1964.

Hayden, Clifford. "MI/DAC Cuts Fleet Costs," *Diesel Equipment Superintendent*. October, 1966.

"Here's a Tailored Approach to Cut Relamping Costs," *Mill and Factory*. June, 1967, p. 62.

IBM Industrial Development. "DART — Dynamic Automatic Rescheduling Technique for Federal Government Maintenance and Overhaul," IBM, 1965.

IBM Technical Publications. "Plant Maintenance Management System Design Manual," IBM.

IBM Technical Publications. "Plant Maintenance Scheduling at IBM Rochester." IBM.

Jorgensen, George. "What the Computer Can Mean to Maintenance," *Mill and Factory*. March, 1966.

Lewis, Bernard T. *Controlling Maintenance Costs.* Waterford, Connecticut: Bureau of Business Practices, 1964.

"Maintenance Control Thru Data Processing," *Commercial Car Journal*. December, 1964.

"MI/DAC System Keeps Close Eye on Lily Tulip's Lubrication Schedules," *Paper Trade Journal*. June 20, 1966.

Mill and Factory. June, 1967, p. 42.

Monson, R. C. "Computer Schedules Preventive Maintenance Work," *Plant Engineering*. January, 1967, p. 129.

Morin, Robert. "Maintenance Costs Held Down by Preventive Maintenance Scheduling and Machine by Machine Cost Records," *Mill and Factory*. February, 1966, p. 57.

Paletti, A. V. "Data Processing Equipment in Evaluating Maintenance Operations," *Techniques of Plant Engineering and Maintenance,* Vol. XV. New York: Clapp and Poliak, Inc., 1964, p. 72.

Rohan, T. M. "Punched Cards Put Maintenance Under Tight Cost Control," *Iron Age*. September 5, 1963.

Santner, A. J. and M. D. O'Hern. "How to Switch Preventive Maintenance to Data Processing," *Mill and Factory*. July, 1965.

Smith, William J. "Data Processing by Machine," *Maintenance Engineering Handbook,* 2nd Edition. New York: McGraw-Hill, Inc., 1966.

Spitzer, Herman. "Low Cost EDP Provides High Preventive Maintenance Reliability," *Plant Engineering*. November, 1967.

Ulahos, C. J. "Computers: Maintenance Management's Sharpest Cost Cutting Tool," *Mill and Factory*. June, 1967, p. 41.